Farewe

Farewell to Mayo

AN EMIGRANT'S MEMORIES OF IRELAND AND SCOTLAND

Sean Ó Ciaráin

BROOKSIDE

The typesetting of this book was produced
by Gilbert Gough Typesetting, Dublin for
Brookside, 2 Brookside, Dundrum Road, Dublin 14.

ISBN 1 873748 00 0

Printed in Ireland by
Colour Books Ltd, Dublin

For the late Donall MacAmhlaigh
and the late Dominic Behan

Contents

Preface

THIS IS NOT A book of fiction or fantasy but a true record of my own experiences, feelings and thoughts throughout my early life. There are no figures of the imagination in this book, but real flesh and blood people who played their parts, however brief, in the saga of my life's story in Ireland and in Scotland. No superfluous embellishments have been added. It all happened and has been taken down from memory.

Thousands of others who grew up in Ireland before or during the war and emigrated to Britain in the late nineteen-forties or fifties could write similar memoirs, but with the exception of a very few, they have shown a marked reluctance to put their experiences on paper. I decided that I would do so before it was too late, for ours will soon be a diminishing generation. We are getting old, our way of life is all but gone, and before we ourselves go, I feel it to be right that some of us should set down the inside story of our experiences as a document to those who come after us.

CHAPTER ONE

Early Days

I REMEMBER AS A CHILD looking out the window and thinking "isn't there many a house in the world". To me the world was what I could see from where I stood. The blue mountains in the far distance were the end of the earth and I had no conception of anything that might lie beyond.

I can remember things that happened when I was still very young, even back to the time when I had no trousers, only a very long red garment reaching down nearly to my toes, something like a girl's dress—"my coat" I called it. When I saw a shed being built across in Attycunnane and a red roof being put on it I thought it was a coat they were putting on it, like the one I had.

Another of my early recollections is of the time I went with my mother to visit a neighbour, an old woman who was sick in bed. She died soon afterwards and when I saw the funeral passing along the road outside our house, I thought they were taking her to heaven in a long box on the cart. That sort of thing, an unusual happening, can stick in the young mind and is remembered when everyday commonplace things are not.

One day, some time after that, I saw what I took to be another funeral coming up the road, a big crowd of people walking along, except there was no cart with a coffin in it. They stopped at our gate and my mother went out and shook hands with a woman in the front of the crowd. The woman kissed my mother and then she tried to kiss me. But I was not having that. I ran off into the house as fast as my short legs would take me and then I looked out the window. The people outside on the road were laughing at me.

It was a neighbour's daughter going away to America. The custom at the time was for all her friends to go with her for the first few miles of the road on her departure. About thirty years later I saw that same lady home on holidays, or on "vacation" as she called it. I did not mention the incident of the attempted kissing, nor did she. She probably did not remember it. She did say she went very near to have been my aunt. She would have married my uncle only he had no place—no house or land. So she went to America instead.

When I was about five years old my mother had to go away to Castlebar Hospital for an operation for appendicitis. Any surgical operation was regarded as a serious thing in those days. She was taken away in an ambulance and just before she got into it, she came over to where I was standing and kissed me, and I remember her face was wet. Then she got into the ambulance and it drove off. She came back unexpected some weeks later, in a car driven by a man from the town, and she had brought a paper of sweets with her for me. I sat eating them and listening as she told my father how she got discharged from the hospital and came home. The doctor had told her that morning that she could go home and so she took the bus from Castlebar to Ballina and there got the Belmullet bus. He said she was great to have managed it on her own, and I thought so too, because when I heard her say "I took the bus", well, I took her at her word. A bus was that big thing, ever so much bigger than a motor car, that I used to watch coming in the Attycunnane road every evening, and I thought from the way my mother spoke that she had taken one of them and driven it herself. When I told this to Dominick Ruane, who was about two years older than me, he said I was a fool to believe her.

The happenings of the first morning I went to school are as clear to me now, if no clearer, than some of the things that happened yesterday. As the time of my school days drew near my parents worried about how I would cope. This was because I had a bad eye. Due to some inflammatory condition of the face suffered in babyhood, I was left practically blind in my right eye. I had heard a lot about that eye. I hated them to talk about it and I pretended I had good sight in it, which was not true and they knew it. Anyhow, I was nearly seven years old before I started school. My people, for some reason, thought that as I got older the sight would improve as the eye would strengthen. But it did not. This handicap, however, did not hinder my learning in the least; the other eye served me well.

It was a fine morning as I set out with my father to walk the two miles to Shanahee school. We met Edward Padden on the road driving cows. Edward had finished school shortly before. "God help him, the poor fellow", said he when my father told him where he was

12

taking me. "He has many a long day out before him and many a *leadóg* of the cane from Galligan."

That was poor encouragement for me and I was nervous enough without it. By the time we reached the school it would not have taken much to make me turn and run home again to the safety of our house. There was one lad I knew and his father had to carry him on his back for the last half mile on the first morning he went to school. It was a laugh at the time, but I know how the poor frightened child must have felt.

My father knocked on the school door and then took off his cap and waited. This was a new thing to me, this knocking on the door and removing the headgear, and waiting for something to happen. Around our place people never bothered to knock when they came to the door, they just lifted the latch, walked in and said, "God save all here", and whoever was inside answered, "God save you kindly". And the only time men ever took off their caps or hats was when they were going to bed, or in the chapel, and sometimes, but not always, at meal times.

The noise inside in the school ceased and the door was opened by an oldish man wearing no hat or cap and with an almost bald head, school master Mister Martin Galligan. After a few words with him my father went away and I was taken in and placed at the end of the infants' class. Mrs Galligan, the master's wife and assistant, looked after the teaching of the infants, the first class, and the second class in the two-roomed, two-teacher school. Her husband, the principal, taught the higher classes. One of the first things I noticed was the long wicked-looking cane. I knew well what that was for. I had heard about it, and it was not long until I saw it being used, as boys and girls walked up ruefully to Mrs Galligan for their punishment and returned to their places with red faces, squeezing their hands under their armpits and biting their lips, trying not to cry. "I would not please her as much as to let her see me crying", said Anthony McAndrew outside at playtime. Anthony had received four slaps on each hand for not knowing his father's name in Irish.

I got no slaps the first day, but I got my share of them soon enough. "She has a design on you", said Dominick Ruane, and he was right there. She had a design on me all right, almost from the beginning. And it was not a good design. How one stood in that woman's favour depended to a large extent on how one's family fared within the pecking order of the parish. The children of the people who ran the

Post Office were great pets of hers, and if you had a relation a teacher, a civic guard, or better still, a priest, you had it made. None of my family connections had ever reached such high local pinnacles, and so I got scant quarter from Mrs Galligan. I remember the year, when at the beginning of the summer holidays, some loaves of bread that had been left over were being handed out (that was after the bread and cocoa came). Dominick Gaughan and I were the last two in the queue for the share out and there were only two loaves of bread left. She gave me the loaf with the holes in it, where the mice had got at it, and kept the good one for Dominick, who was behind me. His uncle was the local County Councillor. I never forgot that.

During my first days at school I thought the other classroom, the master's room, was about the most terrifying place in the world, from all the ructions and shouting that went on in there. The noise that man made could be heard, not only in our room, but out on the road as well. I thought it must be a hell of a place, but when in the course of time I got moved in there I found it to be much the same as the other room. The sums were harder and they were in Irish—and that didn't help. For the most part I could make neither head nor tail of them. I was never meant to be a mathematician and I suffered sorely for it. One sum wrong, two of the cane; two wrong, four of the cane; three wrong, six of the cane. That was the way for many a day between Galligan and me, and with all the beating I could never learn to do long division. Corporal punishment, in school or anywhere else, has always been, in my view anyhow, a degrading thing, both for the giver and for the receiver. In Shanahee school it was nearly always administered with a cane, also called a pointer. I never saw a belt being used, but I saw the cane been used perpetually. Well do I remember the noise that slim weapon made as it swished through the air and came down to meet pink young flesh with a sickening thud. And the defiant grins on the victims' faces as they tried not to cry out. Often arms and legs were slapped as well as hands and sometimes ears and noses were pulled and twisted as a diversion. One lad, a cousin of mine, was left with a permanently bothersome proboscis, which always swelled up and got sore in frosty weather as a result of the maulings it underwent at the hands of one of Galligan's successors in Shanahee school.

There was always a lot of fighting going on amongst the boys, out in the yard at playtime and along the road on the way home. Feuds flared up over one thing or another and went on for days or weeks until in the end they subsided again. And nobody worried about the rights or the wrongs of the thing; a man's "duty" was to back up his brothers or the lads of his townland, and if he didn't do that he was "not much of a man". The lads always referred to themselves as men and the best fighter was the "best man". I never saw the girls fighting.

The Ballyglass lads were a bad crowd for "firing" stones—pelting them after us when we parted from them at the crossroads. As we, the Morahan ones, made off along the road leading to our townland the stones used to come buzzing around our ears. Injuries were sustained in this manner a few times, followed by visits to the school of angry parents to complain, but the teachers never did anything about it. Galligan said that what took place outside the school gate was no concern of his.

For a long time, it must have run into a year of more, I suffered regularly at the hands of two aggressive and bullyish-minded cousins, in whose company fate had ordained that I travel to and from school. Cousins to each other they were, not cousins of mine. Both were about the same age as I was, but smaller for their years, snotty-nosed little fellows with their socks down around their ankles, and although I could take on either of them on my own, together they were too much for me. They were always picking on me and though things never got so bad as to affect my school work, they were making me feel miserable, and for a while I dreaded going to school on account of them.

"They would not do it to me", said Thomas Davitt. They would not dare try, for he had nine brothers, between big and small—I had none. "Two against one would kill a good man", said Pete Philbin by way of commiseration one day after I had taken a beating. I did not want to get killed so I had to do something. I took a leaf out of the Ballyglass lads book—I resorted to the stones, a thing I had often been warned against at home—never throw stones. But as I said, I had to do something. So I "fired" the stones.

The first time I remember this to happen was one evening on my way home, after I had hung behind for a while, playing with Jackie Ginnelly, but really trying to avoid a confrontation with them. I knew they were waiting in ambush for me; I could see them sticking up their heads from behind the whin bushes to see if I was coming. It was at the mearing between Morahan and Shanahee, a quiet place with no houses nearby, and one of their favourite spots for picking a fight with me. But the worm had turned out of sheer desperation. I

15

had my pockets full of stones and as I approached the ambush position I started firing them. I have often heard that sometimes attack can be the best means of defence and it was with me that day. When I started flinging the stones my enemies got up and fled in haste, shouting back dire threats about what they would do to me on the morrow. "We'll leave a scum on the other eye for you."

True to their promise they attacked me again on the way home the following day, and this time they made sure it was hand to hand at close quarters. They knocked me down on the road, and as the kicks came in, I grabbed one of them around the ankles and brought him down along with me, but not on top of me; he fell flat on his back. Then I managed to get to my feet and I broke free and ran with the two of them in hot pursuit, but they did not catch me. I made my way home across the fields. I did not tell in the house about what was going on.

Another encounter another day, this time with one of them on his own, ended with him having an induced nose bleed and his two sisters making a great fuss, putting him lying on the green and shoving a white stone down his back, and warning: "Johneen Carey, if anything happens to Patrick, you're in trouble", and "don't mind who hit who first, you hit him last", and "the fighting will have to stop".

The fighting did stop, but not before another few scrimmages took place. And I was gaining confidence. I had found out they were by no means as brave as they made themselves out to be. The more I stood up to them, the less they forced the issue, and whenever one of them was without the other, he wasn't brave at all. Gradually hostilities ceased and we became friends. All was forgiven, but never fully forgotten, not in my mind anyhow. It has always remained in my memory.

CHAPTER TWO

Growing Up

ABOUT THE SAME TIME as I started school I also started to walk the four miles every fine Sunday to Borhauve Chapel to Mass. Initially, I went with my father, but soon I grew out of that and went on my own, or often in the company of one or more of the other boys of the townland. To our elders we were not known as "boys"; to them we were "Gasoors", "the Gasoors of the village"; never "garsoons", as I believe boys were called in some parts of Ireland.

First Communion day was a great and holy one for us, as it was and is for Catholic children everywhere. It was preceded at school by much preparation, so as to make sure we knew exactly and correctly both how to confess our sins and receive the Sacred Host. We were strictly obliged to have fasted from the previous midnight. No food, no nourishment of any kind was to have passed between our lips under pain of sacrilege, and should anybody break that rule, they were committing a mortal sin, and punishment for that was hell, damnation for ever. It is different now. Nowadays you can have breakfast an hour beforehand and then go and receive Communion, and it's no harm at all. I wonder did people go to hell for it in the old days, if we can get away with it now? Somehow, I don't think so. I would say it was all a big kid on.

Confirmation too was another great event. For weeks we had been drilled and cross-examined on catechism. We had to learn that little book from cover to cover. We had to learn it off by heart and we were examined and re-examined on it from every angle. My wife said that in her place they were forced to learn it by heart backwards. I don't remember them carrying it to that extreme with us, but they carried it far enough I can tell you. It would be a terrible thing, we were told, should any of us not have the correct answers to whatever questions the bishop might ask us. He might put us out of the chapel in disgrace.

When at last the great day came the dreaded man turned out to be a kindly old man and easy to get away from. The question he asked me was, "who are the people who go to Heaven?", and I replied "the good people". So that was it. That was all there was to it after all the fuss. And everyone was confirmed; not one person was turned away. I remember thinking, "wouldn't it be nice if we were all to die now, we would go straight to Heaven".

Twice yearly, in March and in September, we had the stations in our townland. That was when the priests came to some house to say Mass and to give absolution and Communion to the people, a custom which came down to us from the bad old times when chapels were few and far between. Stations were held on a rotary basis—a different house was chosen each time until the whole townland was covered, and then they started again at the first one. The parish priest always announced at one station whose house they would come to next time round, and it was considered unlucky not to accept them. I knew people who were unconventional enough to do just that—they postponed the stations, using the plea that they had a bad house or some other excuse, and I did not notice them having any worse luck than before.

A collection was always taken at the stations, one of several collections the people had imposed upon them throughout the year. The priests were seldom backward in claiming their monetary dues. There was a "curates' collection" for the two junior priests; a "youngsters collection", with donations from the unmarried rather more than from the young; and collections at Christmas and at Easter and at other times in between. The name of each person and how much they contributed was read out loud by the priest for all to hear; for example, "Anthony Carey two shillings, Patrick Gaughan, two and sixpence", and so on to the end of the list. And that was a practice that encouraged people to give, as it was meant to, but it was very humiliating for poor people who could afford to give but little.

At school the Galligan team, husband and wife, moved away to Achill, and the new principal was Mr Seán Duffy, a Ballina man. Duffy was a much younger man than Galligan and a great football enthusiast—a GAA man. He tried to organize a school team more than once, but it was not a success, it never properly got off the ground. Somehow I think we were not good material for a football team. His assistant teacher was Miss Cafferkey, but she did not stay with us for long, and after her we had a succession of "Misses", a Miss Walsh, a Miss McDonagh, a Miss Cassidy, and others who all came and went inside a few years. The man teacher was always known to us as "the master" and the woman was "the missus".

I finished my schooling under Duffy, and though he was a severe man in the school, I always respected him. I found him to be a fair man, and pleasant too if one met him outside school hours. He was free and liberal with the cane, but what teacher of his time was not? I do not know what their views on capital punishment were, but by the Lord they were strong on corporal punishment, those teachers of the nineteen-thirties.

The parish priest was the manager of the school. Whenever he came he would surely question us on catechism. One day he asked Tom, the lad who sat next to me, to say the ten commandments. I am not going to give Tom's surname now, but he was from Shanahee, and he was in the same class as I was. Tom stood up and started reciting the commandments for the priest, and he did very well until he came to the ninth. That was when he made his mistake. "Ninth, thou shalt not cover thy neighbour's wife", he intoned, repeating the words as he always said them. He was not aware there was anything wrong in how he said it, nor had the teacher ever noticed that he had that one word amiss. He was saying "cover" instead of "covet": and that one word made a difference, though not that much really come to think of it—you could say they were related. The priest noticed the deviation at once. He wasn't slow, and he asked Tom to repeat the words. Tom did so, in the very same way as before only more slowly. "Is that how you have been taught to say the commandments, Tom?", asked the priest looking round at the teacher, and his face had reddened back to his two ears. "Yes, Father", replied Tom. The master was standing near the fireplace. The priest said nothing, but if looks could have knocked a man down, Duffy would be on the floor. For a moment he looked as if he was about to attempt to go up the chimney, and I think he would gladly have done anything just to get out of there. Then the priest explained quietly and gravely to Tom that the proper word was "covet", not "cover", and never to say it that way again.

I was sure Tom was for a clouting after the priest left. But nothing happened. The matter was never mentioned again. When I told my people at home about Tom having said to the priest that people should not be covering their neighbours' wives, they thought it was a great joke, and had a good laugh about it. My father even repeated it to some of the neighbours. I did not know at the time where the joke was or why it was so funny. I was to find that out as I grew older.

Another regular and, where some were concerned, not very welcome visitor to the school, was the Guard, who called about once a month to check on the attendance and to admonish bad timekeepers. He used to threaten to send them to a place called Letterfrack— an industrial school in Galway. That was where they would find themselves if they kept on missing days off school, he would tell them. Yet he never got round to having any of them charged, never mind sending them away. He was a man by the name of Cullen, a Donegal man. Often I had a drink in his company in later years, when I was grown up and no longer afraid of him. I was working on the building of Kincardine Power Station in Fife, in the nineteen-fifties, when a fellow worker told me that Guard Cullen was dead, and I felt genuinely sorry, for he was a man I liked. He had served as a Guard in Belmullet for over twenty years and stayed on there after he retired, and I never heard anyone say a bad word about him, only good.

The big bogey man altogether, the man who we were led to believe was going to do shocking things when he came to the school, was the Inspector. Oh, what that man was not going to do! By the way the teachers talked about him, you would think he was going to pull down the roof. They had us in terrible dread of him. Yet the few times he did show up, which were not very often, the man was nothing at all like as bad as he was made out to be. He neither shouted, used the cane, pulled ears or noses, nor pushed people about. The teachers themselves were, I think, as much, if not more afraid of him as we were. And if you were to see the carry on of Duffy, the antics of him behind the Inspector's back, where he would always contrive to be, making signs, trying to convey to us the answers to whatever we were being asked. But when I got found out doing something similar, giving the tick-tack to Dennery, who did not know the answer to what he was being asked one day, I got six wallops of the cane for it, which left my hands blistered and sore for days. Yet Duffy himself was not above doing it when it suited him, on the day the Inspector was there, because he wanted us to have the right answers so that he would get good marks. There were no flies on Seán.

As I advanced into the higher classes (sixth was the highest in the school) I found the teaching of most subjects through the medium of Irish to be more than a little frustrating. The position was that we were rhyming off all sorts of things in Irish, parrot fashion, without knowing properly what they meant in English, and I don't think that was right or to our advantage. English was our first language, the language we had from the cradle; it was the language we done our thinking in, and it was not fair to be teaching us our school subjects in a language which we did not understand. Now let nobody get me wrong. I have as much regard for the Irish language as anybody. I think the Irish people should love and cherish the Gaelic tongue, and learn to speak it, as should all branches of the Celtic race. It would be a great pity were it to die out. But to teach the children their school subjects in it when they don't fully understand it, that is something else. When I asked a teacher at school to tell me the meaning in English of something we were learning in Irish, she said, "Ná bí ag cainnt Bearla" meaning, "don't be speaking English". I was to learn it in the Gaelige and never mind about the Bearla. So I did, and then I did not know what it meant in either language. For all the good it did me, I would have been just as well off not to have gone to the bother of learning more than half of what I got at school. A lot of my time at school was wasted in that way.

In all the schools at that time Irish figured large on the curriculum. The idea was to make Irish the everyday spoken language of the country—a beautiful dream, but one that can never be fulfilled. English got too much of a grip on our people. Also, English has more going for it than the Gaelic has. It is an international language, spoken and used all over the world, something the Gaelic can never be. The English language is in Ireland to stay and that is a fact, regardless of whether we like it or not. But I do not see why Ireland should not have the two languages—that would be a nice thing.

There was one subject above all others I would have dearly loved to have learned in a way that I could understand it, and that was the history of Ireland. But what I found out about it at school left a lot to be filled in. We were well enough versed in old ancient Celtic mythological lore—the Red Branch Knights and the Fianna, and Cúchulain and Queen Maeve—through stories and poems about them in our English reading books. But history proper was taught to us in a random sort of way, and mostly in Irish. It was called "stair" and that was the stair I hated. All I could deduct from it after my best efforts was that the brave, noble, gallant Irish had always been betrayed and foully defeated, just as they were on the brink of wresting their freedom from the cruel brutal English who had invaded their land. And the nearer it got to our own time, the hazier it became, until it all stopped abruptly in 1921. We never heard a word of what happened after that.

I finished school the day I was fourteen years of age. I had never yet seen a bathroom, or a flush lavatory, or running water from a tap. Water for tea and for drinking was fetched in buckets from the well, *Tobar na h-Aille*, at the foot of the cliff. Water for all other purposes came from the barrel under the down pipe from the eave run. Our house had three rooms, counting the kitchen. It wad built in 1924 with the aid of a Land Commission grant of sixty pounds and it had a roof of large diamond shaped slates, and in spite of all the patching and repairing my father and others did on them with mastic and other concoctions, those slates never fully kept out the rain.

Most of the houses in our area in my youth were thatched with straw or rushes or a mixture of both. The house building programme in Ireland did not really get under way until the mid nineteen-thirties and from then on the thatched houses became fewer and fewer, except in the war years, when building was held up for want of materials. And those thatched houses were cosy and warm to live in, far more so than some of the slated houses. Some people kept farm animals in the far end of the long kitchen. It was a commonplace thing in my school days to go into a house of an evening and see the woman of the house milking the cow in the end of the house. I never saw beasts kept inside in the slated houses other than a hen and clutch of young chickens, or on very rare occasions a sick calf or bonham—and of course the dog and the cat.

CHAPTER THREE

Ways and Means

WHEN I WAS A YOUNG LAD growing up I knew no idle times. My work was cut our for me from the time I came from school in the evening until nightfall, sometimes until after nightfall, and sometimes until bedtime. There was always something needing to be done, and what it was depended on the time of year it was. In spring it would be putting out the stable manure on the land for the tillage or for top dress for the meadow, or drawing the seaweed from the shore. In summer it was nearly always the turf I was at, spreading it and footing it, or putting it out on the road for sale, or drawing it home for the winter stack. I was always working with the ass and *bardógs* in those days. I spent so much of my time walking behind the ass I developed a permanent stoop from looking at his heels.

In those days there was no tractor, motor car, or any other mechanically-propelled vehicle of any kind in the townland of Morahan. There were several horses and carts, and one mule, a bad tempered animal, owned by Michael Togher. But every household had a donkey, better known as an ass; some had two or three of them. The ass was an animal with no status symbol attached to him, even the tinkers had them. We had a good little black ass that my father bought as a foal from Pat Keenaghan, for, I think, five shillings. "The Black Eagle" we called him, after a famous race horse of the time. And that eagle was one hardy little beast. Many a lorry load of turf he put out off the bogs on to the road for sale, and many a good stack he took home for the winter's fire, not to mention all the dung and seaweed he carried, and all in the *bardógs* on his back. He and I worked many a long day together. We saw good days and bad days in each other's company. Like myself, he knew no idle times and he died in 1946, worn out by a lifetime of hard work. He was seventeen years of age.

For a number of years we kept a breeding sow, and a contrary animal she was; very protective towards her young, and vicious if a

23

stranger went near them. But her young were always taken away from her and sold after a few short weeks and then she became dangerous and destructive for a few days and had to be securely locked up. Whenever we had the bonhams (piglets) for sale Johnny Barrett used to give us the loan of his donkey cart to take them to town with the Black Eagle, to sell them at the fair. The price of the bonhams and the price of the turf we sold, that was about the only income we had until my father got the dole.

Some families around our place made a living from selling turf with horses and carts. Four shillings per horse cart was what the turf fetched in Belmullet in the thirties and early fourties. I knew men who took two carts of turf into the town to sell every day of the week, the whole year round except on Sundays and holidays of obligation. A lot of hard work went into the turf before it was ready for sale. It had to be cut and saved and put out on to the road, and the weather conditions were not always favourable or anything like it. Often in wet weather the bogs became so sodden that no donkey could travel them, and then people carried the turf to the road on their backs in bags or in creels. I helped with this when I was very young—filling the creels on the bog while my father carried them to the road.

My father was able to make creels, ass's *bardógs*, and *cishawns* (baskets) from the osiers or sally which he grew in the garden beyond the house. The baskets he made were of a flatish oblong shape and were used mainly for holding potatoes. After the potatoes were boiled the contents of the pot would be emptied on the the basket with a bucket underneath it, into which the water was strained. Sometimes on winter nights he made creels and baskets for neighbours. The only payment I ever saw him receive for this handiwork of his was an ounce of tobacco or a bottle of stout. He would have liked to have taught me the wattle-making and he made a few attempts to do so, but I had little aptitude for it, and he was not the most patient of mentors where a slow learner was concerned. Anyhow, the craft is about as dead as a dodo now, so I suppose I did not miss out much in not having learned it. But, like many other things, it's sad to see it gone.

The wickerwork was nice when it was new, but it was not of long enduring quality, and after one season's work, it begun to decay and break up. Strong wooden boxes lasted far longer for rough heavy work such as transporting turf or stable manure on the back of man or ass.

24

Many a time I watched the people on Saturday mornings passing along the road on their way to the town for the week's groceries—the women wearing thick heavy brown or black shawls and some of them carrying baskets of eggs to sell. The men did not carry the baskets, nor take anything to do with the selling of eggs; that was strictly a woman's job and no man would be seen to do it. But if a man had a horse and cart with him he would take the basket of eggs on the cart, often taking neighbouring women's baskets as well as his wife's.

People were far more self-sufficient in those days than they are now. Every household produced its own eggs and its own butter, made in the old dash churns. Most households sold eggs and some sold butter. One who had a good reputation for both eggs and butter was Joyce's of Aughalasheen. They were noted for the fine quality butter they sold to McIntyre's Stores and anyone wishing to buy country butter there were advised by the foreman, Tom Leonard, to buy "Joyce's butter, the best in the west". Groceries bought by the country people were mainly tea, sugar, and tobacco, with fish, usually herring or mackerel, for everyday kitchen. Meat was only bought on special occasions and a loaf of baker's bread was a treat. Flour for home baking came in eight stone bags, brought home on a cart or across the ass's back. It was different of course with the townspeople, they had to buy lots of things which we did not, including Joyce's butter.

The August fair in Belmullet, on the fifteenth, was the big day of the year for taking the country children to town. That was a day to look forward to—"Lá Na Leanbh"—one of the highlights of the year for us young ones. Fairs were always held on the fifteenth day of every month, except when the fifteenth fell on a Sunday, then the fair was on the following day, the sixteenth. Every fairday, street traders and various kinds of hucksters came from Ballina and Crossmolina selling second-hand clothes and diverse other wares. Cattle and pig jobbers came from Tyrawley and up the country, some even from as far away as the Six Counties across the border. All day long from early morning until dusk the town was alive with haggling and bargaining, with the lowing of cattle and the bleating of sheep, and the squealing of bonhams, and the bawling of traders, all going together. It was a great outing for the children to get to the fair, and especially on the fifteenth of August.

At that time the people's way of life was far removed from what it is today. The women often spent the long pre-bedtime hours of the winters' nights, and parts of the days as well, carding and spinning the wool shorn in summer by the men from their own sheep. Almost every house had a spinning wheel and most of the women were expert spinners. The rich woollen yarn thus produced was used not only for knitting (they were splendid knitters too), it was also made up into warp and weft and taken to the local weaver to come back a few weeks later as homespun flannel, tweed, or blankets.

Robert Nealon of Tipp was a weaver, and though a very nice man in every respect, he was not reckoned to be particularly good at his trade. My grandparents, Anthony and Honor Murray, usually took their threads across the harbour by curragh to their near relation, Martin Murray of Gortmelia. I saw several examples of both men's work and the material turned out by Murray was definitely of a superior quality to that of Nealon. Murray's cloth was of a tightly woven fabric, and therefore more hard-wearing. Nealon's was more loosely woven and softer, not as good a cloth. My father had a suit in the nineteen-forties, made by tailor Campbell in Belmullet from grey herring-bone tweed woven by Martin Murray from the wool of our own sheep, and it was a beautiful suit, though he did not like the trousers of it—too narrow in the bottoms, I think he said they were. Wide bell-bottom trousers were the go then. His uncle and cousin, both called Pat Walsh, father and son, had suits woven by Nealon at about the same time, and my father's was by far the best suit of the three, not that the poor men ever had many suits, but they had some nice ones. Although both Nealon and Murray each had several sons, none of them became weavers. When the old men died the family trade died with them. They were, as far as I know, the last two weavers in Erris.

Martin McIntyre and Geoffrey Hurst were the two big leading men in Belmullet in those years, the two big merchants. Most of the country people were in the books of one or the other of those two, for goods received—waiting to sell the turf, or the pig at the Christmas fair, to settle the score. And it was said that they preferred people not to clear the book fully, because while you owed them something, they had you in their power. They used to buy the stacks of turf we had for sale and take it away in their lorries to resell at a good profit up the country. Most people had no option but to sell to the man in whose shop they dealt, as they nearly always owed him money. My father did not believe in getting into debt if he could at all help it. "Better go to bed hungry than borrow", he used to say, because then you could sleep content and independent, without owing anything to anyone.

Selling the stack of turf on the road was handy for people like us who had no horse or cart to transport it to customers in the town. In fact, it was about the only way we could sell it; and besides the bonhams it was one of the few ways we had for making a few pounds.

In the fall of 1937 my father bought a small grey pony foal from a Murphy man in Glencastle. He must have been coming up in the world when he could do that. Seven pounds, I think, was the money he paid for him. And a couple of years later we got a cart, made by James Sweeney of Belmullet. Then we started selling turf by the cart-load to the town people, the same as the men with the big horses and carts were doing, and some of them were not very thankful to us, because as the pony cart was smaller, we were able to sell the cart-loads cheaper and we got plenty of customers. For a number of years we supplied turf to several people in the town, including Austin Gaughan's Bakery, the tailors Barrett and Campbell, and one Dan Maher, a lame man who kept a saddler's shop in Quay Street where he made and repaired horses' harnesses. He made the pony's harness for us and we paid him in kind, with turf—an arrangement that suited both sides.

Although Belmullet town is six miles by road from our house, it is only one and a half miles as the crow flies. By crossing the strand at a place called Morahan ferry, the journey to and from the town can be shortened by three quarters. Even though the tide never dries out fully there, it can easily be forded at ebb tide—on foot, or even with a horse and cart by people who know where to cross (there are more places to cross than one), and who are familiar with the movements of the tide. But for a person without such knowledge, attempting to cross there could be a suicidal business and it cost more than one man his life in times gone by. In my young days, men and women could be seen wading across there almost every day of the year, in all kinds of weather, sometimes waist deep, and modesty dispersed with, for everything was to be seen. And it was a bone-chilling experience on cold winter days. Nobody goes across there any more. No need for a short cut across the water now, when they can cover the six miles in almost as many minutes in their cars. Many a time I crossed it on foot and with Dick, the pony, and a cart of turf.

Although I took many a cart of turf to the town, I can't say I ever handled any of the money. My father himself looked after that part of it. I never even got pocket money. The only revenue I ever had from any source until I was old enough to draw the dole, was the one shilling and sixpence my uncle Pat paid me every Saturday evening for milking his cows. Pat was a bachelor at the time, a hard-working man in early middle age and a man who enjoyed life. Saturday night was his night out, the night for getting dressed up and going off on the bike into the town for a pint with the boys or to meet the girl; he was never short of a girlfriend. So I milked the cows for him every Saturday evening and he paid me one and six for it. It wasn't much, but it kept me going moneywise, for my wants in that line were few—the odd sixpence for a dance, and I always had that and more. Thanks to Pat and the milking I never had to steal potatoes from my people to sell clandestinely for pocket money, like some of the youngsters I knew.

CHAPTER FOUR

People's Entertainments

IN THE YEARS WHEN I was growing up people made their own entertainment. They had neither radio nor television. A gramophone in a house was a rarity, usually having been taken home by someone who had come from America. And the house with the gramophone was a centre of entertainment. Some houses were noted for the good crack that went on in them; they were "visiting houses", where neighbours gathered nightly and talked around the fire. And some of those neighbours were good talkers, with no shortage of interesting things to talk about. The older generation remembered the days of the Land League (my grandfather had seen Michael Davitt, the founder of the League, and heard him speak), and they were well able to relate the traumas of that time: to tell about the evictions, and the resistance to evictions; of how the people chased the landlord's cattle off his farm on to the roads with dogs, and finally chased the landlords themselves, and even shot a few of them; and about how the grabbers were dealt with, and so on. Two of the older men in our townland, Ned Dixon and Ned Gaughan, had been imprisoned for their activities during the agrarian troubles.

The excesses of the Black and Tan period, and of the Civil War, were still fresh in people's minds; especially the letter, which had left an aftermath of enmity and bitterness that divided neighbours, and in some cases brothers, as it did all over the country. I remember well the 1932 general election. That was when de Valera came to power. My father and my grandfather were delighted as they were both de Valera men. It was after that that the people got the dole and from then on there was always a few shillings coming into the houses every week. Also, we got free beef for a while. Every man drawing the dole received a voucher every week entitling him to a certain amount of beef for nothing; how much beef he got depended on the number of dependants he had. This came, I believe, as a result of the "economic war" with Britain, when a tariff was imposed on the export of cattle, causing prices to drop to almost nil. We enjoyed the free beef while it lasted. It was the first, and amongst the best good feeds of beef some of us had ever had. That period might not have been good for the cattle farmers, but it was a godsend to the likes of us. There is an old saying, "It's an ill wind that favours nobody", and it proved itself a true saying then.

Some of the old people I knew had a wealth of oral folklore, going back a long time, to the time of the Spanish Armada and beyond. Around the winter turf fires I heard stories told by people who had never read a book or a newspaper, and who were not even able to read or write—stories about big ships that had been wrecked on the rocks, "fad fado", long long ago, and about bodies having been washed ashore of men wearing grand jewellery and of how the fingers had to be hacked off to get the rings, which in turn were taken from the people by Bingham's men; not the Bingham of Elley Castle, but another earlier Bingham, Richard Bingham, an ancestor, I believe, to Lord Lucan of more recent fame.

The old people believed there was gold from a wrecked ship lying at the bottom of Broadhavan Bay, guarded by a sea serpent—"péist mhara"—and that a chest of gold coins had been buried at night near Inver by a foreign seaman, who took his bearings from the positions of the moon and stars on that night long ago, and they had never been recovered. They had folk memories of the Vikings, or the Danes as they always called them; they said they came in their boats from the sea and stole the women, and that they were able to make "drink" from the heath. But the secret of that got lost; the last man who knew it jumped down the cliffs and committed suicide rather than reveal it.

The prophecies of the Erris seer, Brian Rua Carabine, were often recalled, as were those of St Columbkille. Denis Cleary of Ballyglass was an authority on Columbkille's. Originally a Ballycroy man, Denis's forbears had, it was said, access to some very old writings from Donegal, whence the family had at one time come and where they had, in the days of the old chieftains, been scribes to the O'Donnells.

Peter Barrett of Morahan, who died in 1938, was a prolific reciter of the works of the Erris poet Dick Barrett, who, amongst other things, was active in the United Irishmen in 1798. Peter could, I would think, keep singing Dick's songs and reciting his poems for a month without repeating himself. Nearly every old man or woman

30

you would meet had stories about the misdeeds and the depradations of Major Bingham, who lived in Elley Castle in the late seventeen-hundreds. He was, by all accounts, a chaser of both priests and women, but with different purposes in mind. He was largely responsible for the arrest of Father Manus Sweeney, who was hanged in public from the market crane in Newport. Also, there was a goodly store of local folklore concerning the famous Dean Lyons, parish priest of Kilmore-Erris at the same time as the Major ruled from Elley. And from what I used to hear the Dean was a man who was able to put the Major in his place when he had to; evidently he had friends in very high places. Dean Lyons had a chapel and a dwelling house in Shanahee; parts of the remains of both were still to be seen in my youth.

In those days or rather in those nights of my youth, dances were often held in the country houses. A long thatched house was considered ideal for dancing in, all the better if it had a concrete floor. Many of the old houses had flagged stone floors and they were not so good for dancing. Yet people must have had to make do with them at one time, when there was no better, but I suppose they did not mind because that was all they knew.

Every winter, one or more "school dances" would be held in the district. By way of explanation, a "school dance" as we knew it had nothing whatsoever to do with the school. It was a chain of dances lasting a whole fortnight, with dancing in a different house every night for the duration, except on Saturday nights when there was none; this was to give the people a chance to be up in time for Mass on Sunday. Those dances were usually run by two musicians, a fiddler and an accordian player, but sometimes by one man on his own. On the second last night of the fortnight the musicians collected their dues—one shilling per person from all who had attended. They shouted out the names and each person came up and paid as his or her name was called. As far as I know the people who placed their houses at the school dances' disposal got no remuneration in money, but they were always publicly and profusely thanked by the musicians at the fortnight's end.

An old fiddler by the name of Michael Doogan, a native of Cornboy, spent the winter months for many years travelling around the Erris countryside running school dances. He was a crabbit old fellow and because he was so crabbit he often endured a lot of pranks and teasing from his clients. The young crowd were like that, when a man was contrary they played on it. Raffles were regularly held in people's houses, with dancing in the kitchen and card playing—the game of twenty-five—in the room, and all for the modest fee of sixpence. The prize for the raffle was anything from an old horse or ass to an alarm clock. Very often the winner regarded his gain with such triviality that he did not bother taking it home with him and then it might be played over again at a later date. Conor of Tipp had an old ass which he raffled over and over again, six times in one winter, I believe, and he ended up with the animal. Talk about having your loaf and eating it! But I don't think Connor had the ass long, it died before the winter was over.

Those functions usually ended about midnight, when everybody jumped up all at once to go home and then there was a scramble for caps and overcoats. Some of the fellows did not go straight home but "conveyed" their girls a bit of the road first, and maybe loitered along the way, a practice as old as the human race itself.

On Sunday nights, if there were no dances around the area, young people came from the surrounding townlands and congregated at the end of Tipp Road; there to stand and talk, and indulge in horseplay for a few hours, and some to pair off for to court in the haggards or besides the turf stacks. The priests did not look with favour upon this obvious venue for "company-keeping", which according to them was a "great sin". Nor did they always give their blessing to the dances either. They were very much against certain kinds of dancing, for instance, when the partners held each other close. "The intimacy of the embrace" was considered sinful, so you were to watch how you held your partner. However, it was a different story some years later when the priests themselves set up and ran the parochial halls. Then it was in their interest to see the crowds coming and the youngsters could embrace and wench to their hearts' content. They could do as much company-keeping as they liked, and there was never a word said against it, not by any priest ever I knew anyway. As long as the money kept coming in they did not worry, or if they did, they kept it to themselves. It seems that the parochial halls took the sinfulness out of the company-keeping.

The ultimate sin altogether was to allow dancing to go on in one's house during lent. Do that and you were read from the altar, and to be read from the altar made you a social outcast, a pariah in the parish. Anyone that that happened to could not expect to have any luck. It happened to a man in Trista and his cattle died. Personally, I fail to see what was so dreadfully wrong with dancing during lent any more than at any other time, or how it could be such an affront to the Almighty. But we were not to question these rulings, never mind try to understand them. They were mysteries which we were obliged to accept.

The first dance hall I ever heard of was in Geesala, run by an old geezer named McGeehan, a retired school master who had, amongst other reputations, a bit of a name as a womaniser. Hurst in the town was next in on the act; he set up a hall, and then the barber, Frederick James, a Jew, who lived in Belmullet at that time, opened a dance hall as a sideline to his hairdressing business. Before many years several dance halls, or old sheds that passed for dance halls, were operating in Erris. Bands sprung up to supply the music, usually local outfits consisting of one or two fiddle and melodian players and a drummer. Sometimes for a big dance they hired bands from up the country. The traditional sets and reels now gave way to new dances; quicksteps, foxtrots and what have you, and the country house dancing gave way to the halls. To charge money for allowing people to dance in one's house was illegal, and therefore attracted the attention of the Guards, with the result country house dances were raided. In time, the old dancing in the houses faded away and a grand old tradition came to an end.

But the company-keeping still persisted and so concerned did the old canon in Belmullet become about the moral welfare of his flock, he took to roaming the streets at night after the dance halls emptied out, chasing courting couples, or people he took to be courting couples, and beating them with an umbrella. No wonder there was a decline in the marriage rate. How could young people be expected to form relationships and to get to know one another well enough to marry with that kind of carry on?—and Canon Hegarty was not alone in his bizarre behaviour. It was quite the done thing at that time all over rural Ireland for priests to go around flushing out and chasing courting couples. After a while it stopped, the chasing I mean, not the courting. As I said, it took the clergy-run parochial halls to stop the courting from being "a most grievous sin", and "an abomination in the sight of Almighty God".

Matchmaking was only occasionally resorted to in my time. It was losing the popularity it once had, but it was still useful in some cases. The ageing "boy" of forty or fifty who had stayed at home on the land with his parents was often a case for the local matchmaker to take on hands. A man in that position usually made an effort to get himself fixed up with a wife before it was too late entirely, and he was out of his element if he tried playing the field at the dances. He hadn't done that in time or if he had, it had not come to anything and trying it now would only make him a figure of fun in the district as it did to some. So the matchmaker was his only hope.

Old Jimmy Lavelle of Shanahee was a noted matchmaker in our district and many a man he got a wife for. A good, well-stocked holding of land was an asset in getting any middle-aged man a wife. An old father or mother in the house were not, particularly a mother. An old woman could be an awkward customer for a daughter-in-law to come in to live with; in most cases an old man was easier to put up with.

Some of those old stale bachelors were hard to please in the line of a wife. Looking for a young one they would be (and them near pension age), so she would be sure to have children to keep the line going, or if it wasn't that it was a woman with a good dowry they wanted. That kind of a man might have to ask for the hands of a few women before he got one to marry him, because the ones he was after wouldn't have anything to do with him, but if he persevered long enough and kept up his quest, he usually succeeded in the end. As my first girlfriend used to say about ourselves, "every old shoe finds an old stocking". And so it was with the man who went around looking for a woman to marry him. No matter how contrary he was, or hard to please, if he was keen enough and kept on trying the chances were that, unless there was something very far wrong altogether about him, he would get an old stocking for his old shoe in the end.

Matchmaking died hard in Erris. I knew cases where the couples had found each other through the clerically-disapproved company-keeping method, and the parents held a meeting for the purpose of discussing dowry in money or kind, and so forth, even though the young couple was not interested in that side of things. But if one or other party did not like the prospective in-laws, that could be a bad stumbling block in the case of a bride who was coming in to live with parents-in-law. It could be sheer hell. And all too often in cases where the bride was well received the pressure of living with in-laws soon turned things sour, and then there was trouble—"fighting like a bag of cats".

I can well understand the difficulties facing any old man or woman when their son took in a wife to live in the household. It was a bad system for both parties, a system which often gave rise to no end of disharmony. When a couple get married they are far better off with a place of their own, no matter how humble. Newly-married couples living with their in-laws was a bad way, but it was the way in the countryside where I grew up. The son and heir was expected, at some stage, to marry and bring in a wife to the house. But he was not to do it too soon; should he try that he was in danger of being shown the door. He had to wait until the time was ripe, and in a lot of cases that meant waiting too long.

When marriages took place the ceremony was always celebrated in the bride's parish church, often in the afternoon or late evening. I heard my grandmother say that the way in her young days was for the bride to go to the chapel riding side-saddle behind her father on his horse and return in the same way behind her new husband. People who had no horses walked to and from the chapel. I myself saw a marriage party leave Shanahee on foot to walk to Borhauve chapel, a distance of almost five miles. The custom was for the guests to assemble afterwards in the bride's house where festivities went on into the late hours of the night, often until the early hours of the next morning.

A highlight of the wedding evenings, and something, which as far as I know, existed only in west Mayo, was the attendance of "straw-boys" at weddings. They were a colourful, mummer-like uninvited group of locals, mostly young men, dressed up in queer garments such as women's petticoats and men's long johns and wearing masks, known as straw hats, cone shaped things that came down over the head and face and rested on the shoulders—hence the name "straw boys". Those hats were made during the evening in houses near hand from straw from the haggards. My father was an expert at making them. That was one job he would surely be asked to do whenever there was a wedding in the district—to make the straw hats.

A group of straw boys could number anything from ten to twenty or more. They were under the control of a chosen "captain" who was responsible for their good conduct. Having led them to the wedding house he knocked three times on the door and asked permission for him and his men to come in. This being granted they entered in twos at his command and lined up on the floor. He had them numbered in twos: the first two people were "Number One", the second two

"Number Two", and so on, and he called out the numbers of those who were to dance until all had got their turn. There was also a captain's mate but his was not a very active role; it involved no more than sticking beside the captain, and while it was the captain's privilege to dance with the bride, the mate danced with the bridesmaid.

Two others accompanied the "straw-boys", the "Breedoge" (the Biddy) and her old man—two local characters dressed up as an old man and woman. Those two played all sorts of harmless tricks and antics, and they would not say no to a drop of whiskey or a bottle of Guinness. And though they took no part in the set dancing, they could always be depended upon to oblige with a song or a spot of step dancing.

Straw-boy groups were, as I said, mainly composed of young men and youths from around the district, though older men were welcome whenever they cared to come along, and there would nearly always be a few of the more adventurous girls amongst their number. This was not welcomed by some very superstitious people who thought the presence of female straw-boys at a wedding could cause infertility in the bride. The captains took a more enlightened view of this: I never heard of any of them ever barring any person because of sex. But any right captain would not allow anyone to come who was under the influence of drink, or who might be likely to cause trouble. After everybody had danced the straw-boys left, the captain and mate being the last to leave after wishing good luck to the newly-married couple.

The one and only time when I was a captain of straw-boys, I realized, to my embarrassment, that on taking my leave I was addressing the newly-weds as "the young couple", when, in fact, they were anything but that. The bride was in her forties, the groom on the wrong side of fifty.

Honeymoons were unheard of in my young days. Broken marriages were few. The knot, once put on, was there for life: it held fast, for better or for worse, until death did they part. There might not have been much of an outward show of affection, but the marriages lasted, and were fruitful; they had big families.

At the other end of the scale, wakes were great social occasions as well; they were nearly as good as the weddings, and better in one way because everybody could go, no need to be asked. They lasted for about three days and people came from far and near and sat around in the kitchen all day and all night long, smoking and having the crack. The girls sat on the boys' knees and flirted, and dates were made, while the corpse, who had made it all possible, was there laid out on the bed, rosary between the fingers.

In the old days there was a tradition of playing games at wakes—"Hart-a-brog", "Priest of the Parish", and other group games—and it was said to have been terrific fun. But the priests had put an end to that sort of thing before my time. It was not respectful to the dead they claimed, and I suppose they had a point there.

The most common thing I saw going on at wakes was smoking tobacco and drinking tea, and there was always plenty of that. One man, a member or friend of the family, would be engaged nearly full time in filling clay pipes with walnut plug tobacco and handing them round to the company. Plates full of loose cigarettes went the rounds too, while all the time tea was being served in the room. Some worthies came from miles away for the sake of getting plenty of cigarettes and tobacco to smoke for nothing and a good feed of loaf and jam, washed down with strong sweet tea.

The wakes were good in my time, but from the way the old people talked they were nothing compared to what they had once been. For one thing, drink hardly featured at all at them, not like the old days. It had become too dear, people could not afford it any more they said. If they were to know the price of it now they would turn in their graves.

Poteen, the scourge of many backward parts of the west, was only very rarely made in our parish, but there was an abundance of it across the water from us, around the Inver area. Many a time I saw the lights of their fires along the shore over there at night, where they had the stills going. It was rife, and a strong industry, along the coast from Inver down as far as Killala, and inland as well, until a fiery missionary priest, Father Coneely, came and vented his wrath on the poteen makers. He commanded them to destroy the stills, and that was a good thing he did. The poteen destroyed many a man and ruined many a home. It was even known to do funny things to the Guards, as testified by a report published in the papers, of a visiting Chief-Superintendent, who around that time, on paying an unexpected call to a Garda Barracks down around there, found amongst other irregularities, the Sergeant standing in the door, urinating out into the street, and two Guards inside, lying sleeping, drunk after having consumed poteen which they had seized from some illegal distiller.

There was a rather unlikely story, which many people believed, that a man from down about the Carrowtighe area, who had refused to break up his still when ordered to by the missioner, grew a small horn out of the side of his head. I don't know whether he did or did not but if he did, he was not the only horny man around there. It was probably some kind of a cyst the man had, as I heard afterwards that it was removed in Castlebar Hospital.

CHAPTER FIVE

Superstitions

IT'S OFT AND MANY A TIME I think about superstitions and the fears and the beliefs and half-beliefs of the people I grew up amongst; things very familiar to my grandparents and their peers, most of whom, I think, were not sure whether to give them credence or not, but who at the same time wished to play safe and not offend against them.

I believed as a child, having been told so by my elders, that the fairies lived in the old headland fort in Gobadoon, in the commonage down by the shore where we grazed the cattle, and that when they played their wild, lonely, unearthly music anyone lucky enough to hear them was gifted with music ever after. Michael Murphy, when he was a young man, heard their music one fine summer evening at dusk, and sitting outside his house, he accompanied them on his fiddle. And in all the whole countryside there was not to be found the equal of Murphy as a fiddler after that.

I was born and grew up at a time when the age-old superstitions and beliefs were at long last losing the grip they once had on the minds of the people. At one time they were attached to about every aspect of life. "Piseogs" the old people called them. My father used to say they were a legacy from the old pagan times, and of course, the clergy were of the same view.

The people of my grandparents' day were, I would say, inheritors of a culture in which the supernatural had played almost as large a part as the real everyday things of life. And having come as they did from such a background who could blame them for thinking, aye, even insisting, that the old way of things should be respected; that the old unwritten codes were not to be lightly infringed; that it was safer not to break with tradition, wiser not to trifle with the netherworld. As my grandfather, old Anthony Murray, told me when I said I was thinking about digging in the fairy fort to see if I could find anything: "Better leave such things alone."

My aunt believed the fairies were fallen angels, who had been cast out of heaven in Lucifer's time. "And it is said", she used to say, "that if we could see them they are as plenty as the grass." According to her, it all began up in heaven a long time ago, when Lucifer, "the brightest angel in heaven", became so carried away with himself that in his pride he thought he should be equal with God, and when he could not get his own way he rose up against God, and there was civil war in heaven, and a mighty battle was fought there with Michael commanding the forces of the Lord and Lucifer commanding the forces of evil. And Lucifer was overthrown, and he was chucked out of heaven and cast down into hell, along with the bad angels who had sided with him.

Now it seems that while all this was going on, there was a third party of angels who did not take sides. They sat on the fence— stayed neutral, waiting to see how the thing was going to go. And when the war was over they were cast out of heaven too. But they were not sent to hell; they were sentenced to wander this earth until the Great Day of Judgment, when their case will come up again, and we should pray for them, that God in his mercy will allow them back into Heaven. So that is how we have the fairies, "na daoine maitha"—the good people, and they are not to be confused with ghosts or evil spirits. I wonder if there is anything to it?

Superstitions, and beliefs and notions about the supernatural were not confined to the country districts of Ireland, nor for that matter were they confined to Ireland. Every country had them. They were, and to a certain extent still are, to be found all over the world. Ireland had its share and indeed a good share, and the west had more than a good share. Where the real superstitious people were they could carry it to far extremes. There was a man in Shanahee, I knew him well, and when he was on his way to the chapel to get married, a hare ran across the road in front of him. He made the sign of the Cross, turned back, and put the whole thing off. Others I knew, and if an animal urinated when they were in the act of buying it, they would walk away and have no more to do with it. I knew women, and not for a fortune would they throw out water after dark. (That was before people had sinks in their houses.) If one of their hens crowed they killed her at once, believing that a crowing hen foretold bad luck and that by killing the hen the ill-luck could be averted. The cock suffered the same fate should he crow in the middle of the night. Bad luck for the unfortunate birds, whatever about the people.

Some people believed that at the first cock's crow in the early morning dawn the supernatural beings of the night fled. That was the signal, they said, for the dead who were not at rest to hasten back to their graves; and for other spirits to return to their various habitations in the air or below the ground. Second cock crow was another warning, and the third was the final warning for all things not of this world to depart before the approach of God's light. I remember, more than once, been awakened very early by the cock crowing and looking out of the window. In the strange half-light it was not hard to imagine seeing grey spectres scurrying off.

It would be impossible for me to relate half the strange ideas some people around our place had, and though, as I said, the majority did not fully believe in them, at the same time they took care not to go against them. One thing most people did believe and that was that it was extremely unlucky to build an extension westward out of a dwelling house. Anybody who did that, they said, would not live long. One man in Borhauve built a room west out of his house. Well-intentioned friends and neighbours warned him against it; he was taking a big risk they told him. But he just went ahead with his building and laughed at them, thinking they were talking nonsense. He was soon to find out who was right. Within a few years both himself and his wife were dead, and the house with its new extension lay empty and derelict as it is to this day. Others round about, people of the same age group as that man and his wife, died too, but no notice was taken of that. Even some of the people who had warned him died, and they had not built rooms west of their houses. He had, and he died, so according to local opinion it proved the point; it was plain to be seen that building west out of your house was unlucky. As the man said, statistics can be made to prove almost anything.

Lots of people of the older generation had experienced, or thought they had experienced, strange unexplainable happenings of some sort at some time of their lives, and if they never had such an experience themselves they always knew people who had. Animals too, they reckoned, could sense or even see things which humans could not. There could be something in that. From my own experience I know that both the pony and the dog felt uneasy when passing by certain lonely places late at night, but then again I suppose it could be that they sensed my uneasiness and it made them uneasy too.

To hear some of the old people talking when they gathered around the fire in some house on a winter's night, the things they went on with would make the hair stand up on your head. Stories about dead people who had been met on the roads at night, or seen near to their houses, and about all the strange sounds that used to be heard—unearthly crying, and such like. That kind of thing mostly happened in the dead of the night, but not always. It could happen in the daytime too. And it was not always the ghosts of the dead who appeared, ghosts or wraiths of living people could be seen on occasion, and when that happened the right thing to do was to go at once and tell the person whose wraith you had seen, otherwise that person would soon die.

The banshee cried for certain families, mourning the passing of descendants of the old Gaelic race. I knew a woman who claimed to have seen the banshee, an old hag shuffling along the boreen, wailing in a most sad manner, and sure enough, a person of the O'Donoughues died that night. I knew several who heard the banshee and they all said it was a very lonely mournful sound.

People could be put astray at night, lose their way when coming home alone at a late hour, and end up miles away in some other townland. Should this happen a good remedy was to turn your coat inside out. This, it seems, confused the fairies, or whoever it was that caused the person to lose their bearings, and the chances were that once the coat was put on, turned inside out, you found out where you were and made your way safely home. They had stories too concerning children who had been taken away and some false thing left in their place—a being which resembled the child but was not the child, and it did not last long, it soon faded away and died.

These were some of the things that were to be heard, being told and re-told, and, I suppose, added to in the telling, around the winter firesides. And when a few of the old seanachies got together that kind of story-telling could go on for hours and hours, each endeavouring to go one better than the other—to tell a more flesh-crawling and awesome tale than his neighbour, and with the eerie winter winds howling outside around the house for background, it was worse than any horror film; it could really make a person terrified. Many a night I had to go out into the pitch black darkness and make my way home along a lonely unlit country road after listening to such a session, and that was when it would hit me right; that was when I was terrified. Some people said that whenever they were out on their own at night after hearing ghost stories they used to be afraid to look behind them. Not for them the mistake of Lot's wife. And the "cold sweat" used to come out on them, or so they claimed. Well, that was not how it affected me. I was never afraid to look back and I don't remember anything about cold sweat. I would stand and listen for a while, to hear if there was anything coming, and then I would take to the heels and run as fast as I could for a bit, and then I would stand and listen again, and then run again. And all the time a strange tickling feeling around my head, as if the scalp was creeping. I used to be afraid I would meet the dead people of the village, or that some horrible monster might come up out of the sea, or from behind the whin bushes. Lonely country roads and the noise of the winds and the sea can produce strange fears on dark nights even if one had never heard ghost stories.

Two places said to be bad for ghosts and hauntings were the mearings between townlands and the remains of old houses, known as "montrochs". If there was any unearthly presence around the district those were two places where it was likely to be encountered. Dead empty walls within which people once lived, but are now deserted and decayed, undoubtedly have a very lonesome atmosphere about them; places that had once known life and light and warmth, but are now dead and dark and cold have a sad, weird, aura eminating from them which I myself have often experienced. I always felt lonely whenever I passed close to such places late at night. But the mearings of townlands never bothered me.

One thing we were warned against was never to leave a wake-house alone at night. "Don't leave the wake-house on your own", I was often told when I was going to a wake. This was because evil spirits were apt to be lurking about in the vicinity of the place where a corpse was, and anyone leaving there alone in the night was in risk of coming foul of them. I left wakes at all hours of the night and walked home with myself for company and I never met anyone or anything worse than myself. Another thing a person should never do was to carry a pack of playing cards abroad at night because wherever the cards were the devil was never far away. I was guilty of breaking that one too, many times over, and never saw any worse devil than myself.

When I was young I was fond of card-playing, and often I carried the pack in my pocket when I went visiting, so that we could have a game in whatever house we were in. We young ones played cards for buttons instead of money for the simple reason we had no money. And I was lucky at winning the buttons. I had a fine collection of buttons once, won at card-playing; as fine a box of buttons of all colours, shapes and sizes as ever you saw. Whatever became of them in the end I know not. My grandfather used to warn me that I would be going around with the cards at night until it would happen to me like it happened Padraigeen Boylan.

Padraigeen was a man who had at one time lived in Morahan and, like myself, he had the habit of carrying the pack of cards around with him at night. One night he was back in Borhauve, card-playing, his cards with him, and on his way home about midnight the devil attacked him as he was coming along the shore. I know the place well and a lonely place it is, even in daytime. There was no road into Morahan at that time—that was why he was walking along the shore. It was the only highway the people had. And that was where the devil, God between us and harm, attacked him—on the shore, just at the mearing between Borhauve and Morahan. First he attacked him in the form of a man, a big coarse hairy man, but when Padraigeen looked down he saw the cloven hooves and he knew then who it was he was up against. It must have been a bright night when he was able to see him so well. Padraigeen was carrying a stick, and the way he kept the devil off was by making the sign of the Cross with the stick. Every time he made the sign of the Cross the devil retreated for several yards, but he always came back again to the attack and each time more terrible than before. What must it have been like for that poor man, fighting the devil, alone, in the dead of night, on that lonely desolate shore?

Three times the devil changed form. Suddenly, instead of a man he was a dog, a big evil-looking black dog, as big nearly as a yearling calf and with two eyes as large as saucers bulging out of his head. But Padraigeen kept him off with the sign of the Cross. The devil then changed himself into a huge black ball, as high as the wheel of a cart, and giving off a smell like burning sulphur as it kept hopping around Padraigeen trying to run him down, but he still kept the thing away with the sign of the Cross.

Finally, it turned into a ram with an enormous big pair of horns, trying to butt him. But again the sign of the Cross prevailed. The man was so exhausted and worn out that it was on his hands and knees he managed to crawl up to the door of Gaughan's at the ferry. Old Mick Gaughan heard him and he got up and let him in, and after shaking the holy water, he gave him a drink of whiskey, which he had in the house, to revive him. He was not able or too afraid to continue the half mile or so to his own house so he stayed in Gaughan's until morning. And from that until the day he died Padraigeen Boylan never again played cards, never mind carry them at night. It was said the pack in his pocket had turned black and stuck together as if they were scorched and glued; whether that was true or not, he burned them and he never again allowed a pack of cards inside his house.

Shortly after hearing that tale I got the fright of my life on my way home one night when a black thing suddenly jumped out from the side of the road and with one almighty leap landed right up on my back. It was our own dog.

The sign of the Cross was good for keeping the devil away, but better still, the best remedy of all for getting rid of him if he was troubling you, was to hit him with a good splash of holy water. The devil could not stand the holy water. The following story, which I often heard told, goes to show the power of holy water against him.

There lived in the townland of Ballyglass a woman who carried on an extra-marital relationship with one of the coastguards from the nearby station. The man died. Now I don't suppose the affair had anything to do with his death. I did not hear what caused it, but he died anyhow, and after that in bed at night, when the woman and her husband would be doing what married couples do (and sometimes couples who are not married), the coastguard would appear, standing beside the bed in a very angry mood. He must have been a jealous old rascal! Things got so bad that the woman and her husband went to the priest and told him the whole story. After reading an office the priest informed them that it was not the coastguard who was bothering them. It was the devil they had seen. The coastguard was in hell. The priest gave them a bottle of holy water, the water he had blessed when reading the office, and he told them that the next time the thing should appear the husband was to shake some of the holy water on it, and to be sure it made contact.

That very night it came again. The coastguard, or the devil in the form of the coastguard, appeared again as usual standing on the floor beside the bed, demanding to know what was going on in the bed (as if he did not know fine what was going on). The husband had the holy water ready and he did as the priest had advised him to. As soon as the water hit the thing on the floor it changed at once into a black cat and jumped on to the foot of the bed and stood there spitting at them. The man made to shake the holy water again but he found it difficult to do so, his hands felt as if they were tied. With one great effort, and holding the bottle with both hands he flung the contents of it on the cat which let out a blood-curdling scream and disappeared in a flash of fire. The couple were never again troubled by that terrible, evil thing.

In a lighter vein was the story old Peter Barrett used to tell about the man who when searching for his sheep on Morahan hill one summer evening as dusk was falling and who did he meet but the devil carrying a big bag on his back. He must have been a courageous man, and an inquisitive one too, whoever he was, because according to the story he stood talking to the devil and in the course of the conversation he asked him what did he have in the bag.

"That bag", replied the devil, "is full of butter, all of it collected in Morahan, and this is how I come to have it. Whenever a stranger comes to a house and the woman of the house says, 'I would make tea for you, but the devil a bit of butter I have'—whenever that happens", said the devil, "if she is telling a lie then all the butter that was in the house at the time goes to me." So that was how the devil had the big bag of butter.

I relate the following story as I often heard it told. I do not know if it has ever been written down before or if there was a similar story told elsewhere in the country as was often the case with those old tales. But it was once well-known around our district at home.

In Borhauve, on land owned in my time by the Tighe family (I don't know who owns it now), there once lived a young widow with some small children. For a time she had been forced to suffer the unwelcome attentions of a man named Seán Crone, a bad man, a travelling man of some sort who frequented the area and who was often drunk.

Late one night as she was about to retire to bed, her children were already asleep, he came to her door and forced his way in, insisting on staying the night. The woman was frightened and more so when he told her he was going to murder her and the children. He ordered her to go down on her knees and pray as she did not have much time left. The poor woman did as he said; she was helpless, it was late at night and there was no house near ha :d nor anyone to hear her should she cry for help. She made no resistance, only prayed, and she prolonged the praying for as long as she could. Crone kept telling her to get finished, that he wanted the thing over and done with, and he kept sharpening his knife on the hobstone.

Then, just as she was about to finish her prayers, the door opened quietly and a small, bent, withered old woman walked into the kitchen. This intrusion enraged Seán Crone. "Who are you?" he demanded. "What are you doing here?" "Get to hell out of here, whoever you are", he shouted. "No", said the old woman, raising her hand, "you will get to hell out of here". The man also raised his hand to hit her but it fell down by his side. Whatever spell the fairy woman, for that was what she was, cast upon him, he was helpless under it. Not a word did he say; nor did he try either to attack her or to get away from her; he was able to do only what she commanded. He walked out of the house in front of her and down to the river, and there she turned him into an old tree stump (a "blockain"), to lie in that place until the Day of Judgment when he will become a man again and rise to answer for his sins.

That block of wood was still there in the nineteen-thirties, lying submerged in the river, beside where we passed every Sunday on our way to and from Mass. And we believed that it had once been the body of Seán Crone. It was, in fact, part of a pre-historic tree of which there are plenty thereabouts. I often wonder how did that story originate. Did somebody local make it up, or could it be there is a kernel of truth in it? Who knows, but maybe a bad drunken brute named Seán Crone who terrified women ended up drowned in that place by accident or design. The old people I heard telling it believed it literally happened as in the story, but I doubt if anyone would believe it now. And it shows how religion and the fairy lore mixed— the woman's praying brought the fairy godmother to her rescue.

It has been said, and with a great deal of truth, that when the electricity came and lit up the countryside the ghosts and fairies went. Also, and alas, the radio and the television destroyed the art of story-telling, and indeed of conversation in general. Now they have their story-telling and their conversation made for them, instead of making it themselves. It's changed times now—the ways of the old people like the old people themselves are gone, forever.

47

CHAPTER SIX

Ancestors

DRASTIC CHANGES TOOK PLACE in our area as well as all over Ireland in the wake of the Great Famine in the middle of the last century. I often heard it said, and I believe it to be well documented, that there were four times as many people in our parish of Kilmore-Erris before the famine as there were a hundred years after it. The older people often talked about people they remembered from their childhood days, or of people they had heard tell of in their youth, from an older generation still, people with strange-sounding surnames, and some with strange Christian names too, names no longer to be found in our part of the country. "They went away on the free emigration", my grandfather, Anthony Murray, used to say, "they all cleared out."

There was a time when people sailed from Blacksod to America—what years those sailings took place I cannot say, but I do know that at one time a lot of people from around our area walked the eighteen miles to Blacksod and there took ship for America. That was easy compared to what some did. People set out on foot from Westport, crossing the hills from Bangor southwards (there was no road to Mulranny at the time). Others walked the whole way to Sligo, a distance of over eighty miles. They would do anything to get a ship to take them away from their famine stricken homeland. Those poor people carried few belongings, they had no belongings to take. It was said some of them took porridge to eat on the way, and they were the lucky ones, they had the grain to make it from. Others took nothing. They set out, walking, without shoes or change of clothes, and when they got on the boat their hardships were only beginning. A long primitive voyage lay in front of them, unimaginable to people used to travelling today. Some vanished without trace or tidings ever been heard of them again, probably buried at sea, their bodies literally thrown to the sharks. An aunt of my grandmother set out for America and was never seen or heard of again.

It was said that people who travelled alone were often murdered along the way for the sake of the clothes they wore, or for the meagre pittance of money or food they carried, and their bodies buried in the bog. Those were cruel times. Yet the people went away. Not only whole families but whole communities cleared out, leaving only the memory of the strange-sounding names they bore, which still remained for generations attached to the little fields and gardens (gairdeens) where they had once grown their potatoes, and which continued to be called after them by those who were left behind, place-names such as "Fail Maire Ní Airt", meaning Mary Harte's field, or "Gairdeen Adam Roc"—Adam Rock's garden: names which had no meaning for people of my generation.

Sometimes over the years tittles of news had come through, or was invented, about how some of them had fared in the new world, as of one man who made good, got himself an education and ended up a millionaire in a western American city. Or of another, named Mooney, who became a trade union activist, got framed for a crime he did not commit, and suffered long years of imprisonment. But of the vast majority there was never any news, and few, very few, ever returned. An exception was my father's maternal grandfather, a man by the name of Anthony Walsh, originally from Emlabeg or Ardmore. He spent a six-week-long voyage going to America by sailing boat in the eighteen-fifties, served on the Federal side in the American Civil War and, when the War was over, returned to Ireland minus an eye. He acquired the land in Morahan where some of his descendants still live; he married, lived out his life and died there. His blood now runs in the veins of hundreds of people, including myself.

The words I speak, the written line, these are not uniquely mine,
For in my heart and in my will, old ancestors are warring still.

Those words I came across some time ago in a book. They were quoted as having been written by someone called Richard Rowley who lived from 1887-1947. And that is all I know about him. It was after reading those lines that I decided to devote a few pages to set down for those who may come after me the things I know of the origin and lives of my parents, grandparents and kin, all of those forebears whose inherited genes have contributed, for better or for worse, into making me what I am. Not much, I doubt, has ever been written about any of them before.

The last survivor of my four grandparents was my mother's mother. She was the link with the past I was most acquainted with and her name was Honor Dixon. Dixon is quite a common name in Erris. According to one woman I knew, who claimed to be an authority on local genealogy, they are all the progeny of a Yorkshire yeoman who served there in the reign of the first Elizabeth. (He must have done more than his army service!) She may well have been right, stranger things have happened, but then again bearing in mind some of her pronouncements about other surnames, I would not take her word as infallible.

My grandmother's father was Frank Dixon and her mother was Peggy Loftus and they lived in Tipp. At one stage they left there with their family and went to America. So I had forebears on both sides of the family tree who had lived for a time in the States and for some reason or other came back again, for Frank Dixon and most of his family, after some years in America, came and resettled in the old homestead.

My grandmother was in her mid eighties when she died in 1955. She never learned to read or write but she was an intelligent woman with a good memory and was well able to recall things that happened over seventy years before. When young, probably in her early teens, she had travelled to America and across it with her parents and family, a long journey about which she retained many vivid and interesting memories. Her recollections of the Red Indians, which she often recounted to me, were not of fierce warriors and all that, but of hungry, famished people begging for food, their lands taken off them by the white settlers. After some years in Montana the family came back to Ireland. Shortly before they came one of her older brothers, Pat by name, drowned while crossing a river in a boat. Not long after another son was born to her parents and they also called him Pat. They had twelve of a family in all, a not unusually large number in those days. Some of them stayed on in America, but most of the others, including the second Pat, the youngest, ultimately came home.

One of her uncles, a man named Anthony Loftus, was evicted from his small farm in Tipp, not because he was unable to pay his rent, but because he refused to pay. It was at a time when there was considerable Land League activity in the area. Loftus and some others, after withholding their rent for a time, or so the story went, decided on the advice of the priest to come to a settlement with the landlord, who, as far as I know, was one of the Binghams. The others, who also had evictions pending, had their money accepted and were allowed to stay on in their lands. Loftus, noted as a local agitator, was thrown out. He afterwards went to America, to Montana.

His eviction was by no means the end of the matter. The fat was in the fire when a local man who had been living in England came home, took possession of the lands and moved in to live in the house. The weight of the Land League organisation was brought to bear against the newcomer. Branded as a grabber, which indeed he was, he was boycotted by the local community. Clergy and politicians put pressure upon him, urging him to quit, but to no avail. Acts perpetrated by night, such as the destruction of his crops and of his curragh, would have earned the doers long terms in jail had they been found out. But nothing could make the grabber budge; he held on in spite of all. Things were so bad that the police stayed in his house full-time, day and night, for about a whole year, giving him protection. Eye witnesses, who were children at the time, told me in their old age that they remembered seeing him working in his field, with two policemen standing nearby, watching him. He must have been under a terrible strain but he was a man of great tenacity and nothing would make him give in. He held on and reared his family there and lived a long life in the place. In later years after a new generation had grown up the whole bitter episode was forgotten. Loftus never came back to Ireland. He was the last Loftus in Erris.

Honor Dixon was in her early twenties when she married Anthony Murray of Shanahee, a man about ten years her senior. A small placid man, he was well-known for his natural skill of treating sick animals, particularly in cases where an animal was having complications in giving birth. Many a person said he was better than a vet and his services were much in demand for many years, right into his old age. His parents had come from two widely separated parts of Erris, about forty miles apart. His father, whose name was Martin Murray, was a native of Cornboy and his mother, Peggy Gaughan, was from Faulmore. How they came to be married and living in Shanahee I never heard. I remember as a boy going to Faulmore to St Deribla's Holy Well with my grandparents in Sonny Henaghan's car (a great novelty to me at the time), and we called to visit another old man by the name of Ned Lavelle, who was a first cousin of my grandfather and whose daughter, a Mrs Keane, kept a guest house in Faulmore, much frequented by priests.

51

My other grandfather, my father's father, was Michael Carey and he died in 1944 at the age of seventy-seven years. The old-timers in his native Doolough remembered him as "Michael Johnny Vichael" —Michael the son of Johnny, the son of Michael. How come there are so many Careys in Erris (it is full of them), or where they hailed from originally nobody that I ever talked to on the matter seemed to know for sure. Seán Duffy, the teacher, held a theory that they were a Kerry sept to begin with, going back a long way to someone called Ciarr, from whom County Kerry took its name, and that because of some tribal upheavals or troubles they moved north and settled in East Mayo for a time, until again they were forced to move on, and eventually they ended up in Erris on the shores of the Atlantic. On the strength of that idea he changed my name in Irish from Ó Ciaráin to a new fangled Ó Ciarraighe, a departure my father did not reckon much of.

One Brian Carey, a merchant, was said to have been the richest man in County Mayo in his day. And according to the stories handed down about him he did not look the part, he always went around in working clothes with large unpolished boots and a cloth cap that was far too big for him. The old people used to say, "Brian Carey was a man without any pride". His unlikely appearance once caused a porter to eject him from a bank in Belfast. The porter, taking the book by the cover so to speak, thought he was a hobo on the look-out for somewhere to lie down, and him one of the bank's biggest depositors.

Another Carey, and one whose true identity has, I fear, been lost, if it was ever known outside of a small circle, went in for taking pot shots at old landlords. Several shootings which took place in Erris were attributed to him. Denis Bingham, one of an infamous line and a reprobate in his own right where his personal life was concerned, was fired at and wounded near Sraigh crossroads late one evening as he returned from Belmullet by horse-drawn car. His wife and the servant were riding in the car with him at the time, and their presence, it was said, deterred the gunman, preventing him from getting in as good a shot as he might have done; evidently he did not want to endanger the women. Bingham had his own gun in the car beside him but things happened so fast he got no chance to use it.

The attempt on the life of another landlord, Henry Carter, was also made in the evening as he was coming home by horse-drawn car. It happened at the gate of his residence, the two story house at Pickle Point. On arriving at the gate the servant man got down off the car to open it while Carter remained seated. Alarmed by a disturbance in the bushes he suddenly jumped to his feet and that very probably saved his life, for it was at that moment the man fired, and the charge, meant for the landlord's body, got him in the legs instead, with the result he escaped death, but lost a limb. One of his legs had to be amputated.

The man Barrett, who was fatally shot in his own house soon afterwards, was no landlord, only a small tenant farmer. But he was too big in the mouth and that cost him his life. At the fair in Bangor, in a public house, and in the presence of several people, he said he could walk out into the street and lay his hand on the shoulder of the man who shot Carter. That night he was shot dead himself, in through the window, as he was getting undressed to go to bed. He was actually sitting on the side of the bed, taking off his shirt, when he was hit, and his wife and small child were in the bed behind him.

The late Michael O'Donoughue, headmaster of Belmullet vocational school, a man who took a deep interest in the history of Erris, told me that he did his best to get the inside story of those shootings out of the Land War veterans who knew it. But no way would they be prevailed upon to give anything away. Bound by an oath they would never break, they took their secrets to the graves with them.

My grandfather, who was a youth in Doolough at the time, admitted to me that he knew the man who fired the shots and that his name was Carey. He even claimed to have watched him doing target practice and said he was a good shot. I asked him if it was the same man who shot Carter and Barrett and he said it was. He also answered in the affirmative when I asked him if the man was a Doolough man. But that was as far as he would go, he refused to tell me anymore. I doubt if the right inside story of that troubled time in Erris will ever now be fully known.

My great grandfather, Johnny Vichael, left Doolough and moved to Tallaght with his family. When his wife, whose name was Brigid Connell, died, he re-married, to a woman named Sally Barrett. He accidentally drowned one night on his way home from the town when he stepped into the canal at the bottom of American Street, a notorious death trap. A man named Jimmy Donoughue was drowned at the same spot and in almost identical circumstances in my own lifetime. His eldest son, Michael, had at the early age of nineteen married Dinah Walsh, daughter of the one-eyed veteran of the American War and settled on part of the Walsh lands in Morahan.

There he remained for the rest of his life, in an old thatched house beside the sea, a mile away from the road, until the stiffness of old age overtook him and then he moved in to live with his daughter Mrs Gaughan, and it was in her house he died.

He was known as a hard-working man, as a skilful and hardy fisherman, and as an uncompromising republican whose home in its remote setting was often a refuge for men on the run during the period known as the the War of Independence and again in the civil conflict that followed. Towards the end of his life when he was no longer able to read for himself, he loved to sit and listen to me read to him from the newspapers and from my school books. They were the only books we had to read.

I remember his boat well. Many a time I sat in it as a child, making believe that I was on the sea. I can only recall seeing it on the water once. That was when his half-brother, Tom, Sally Barrett's son, who was a cattle dealer, went out to Derrynameel island with my father to collect some yearling calves Tom had grazing there. My grandfather himself was too stiffened up with rheumatism at that time to go with them. It was laid up after that, and for a long time it lay upside down in the garden, serving as a shelter for the hens on wet days, until finally it decayed and broke up.

I never knew my grandmother, Dinah Walsh. She was dead before I was born. I do not know what she looked like as I never saw a picture of her. I don't think many country people got their pictures taken in her day. People spoke well of her, as they nearly always did of the dead, and I believe she deserved it. From what I heard of her she was a quiet, hard-working woman, who devoted her life to her home and family and died in middle age after a long illness. Her Christian name, however she came to have it, was a most uncommon one. I never knew another Dinah in the west of Ireland, nor anywhere else for that matter, but as I mentioned earlier some strange names existed in our district at one time and hers may have come down from former days. It died with her, as none of her descendants have been named after her. Her surname, spelled "Walsh" or "Walshe", is always pro-nounced "Welsh" in Erris, and that is as it should be, because Walsh is a corruption of the name. In Irish it is "Breannach" meaning "of Wales". They were a Welsh-Norman family who came to Ireland and there multiplied and expanded all over the country. Today Walsh is the most common name in County Mayo and the fourth most common in Ireland. The first recorded bearer of the name was a

54

Thomas Fitz-Anthony Walsh (meaning Thomas, son of Anthony Walsh) who came over to Ireland with Strongbow, and to this present day wherever there are Walsh's you are more than likely to find the names Thomas and Anthony prominent among them. My grandmother Walsh's mother was a Mary Togher from Ardmore and through her I have relations, Toghers, around Ardmore yet, though they might not know it, nor care. As the fella said, "it's a bit far back now".

My father who bore the name of his grandfather Anthony, was born in 1897, the second son of the family and the second youngest of five. His older brother, John, the man I was named after, went to America, and after seeing service with the American Army in France in World War I, he died as a result of a street accident in New York, aged thirty-three years. My father himself was a member of the Irish Volunteers, and he came under fire at least once. That was on the night of 28 August 1920, when the whole Company, one hundred strong, were marched down to Ballyglass to burn a coastguard station which had been vacated by its occupants the day before. I have never been able to figure out why it was that one hundred unarmed men were sent to burn down an empty building, when two or three men could easily have done it. And almost every old woman and child around the place knew it was going to happen: in fact some juveniles and others who were not Volunteers at all tagged along to see the fun. Most of the men were not able to get near to the fire and had to content themselves with looking on. Who was it said, "they who stand and watch also serve"? They got a big surprise before the night was over.

On their way home, their work completed and them singing as they cheerily marched along, they were suddenly sent fleeing in all directions by a volley of rifle fire from about half a dozen men, mixed police and Black and Tans, who, guided by the former, men who had been in Belmullet for years and were possessed of good local knowledge, had crossed the ferry on foot at low water, and lay in wait for the boys, behind the cover of a stone wall, to give them a warm reception on their return.

It was a bright night with a full moon shining, and many Volunteers, I heard it said, owed their lives that night to one of the policemen, who, not wishing to see bloodshed, started firing wildly and while the quarry were still a good distance off. Had they been given time to come nearer, and the Black and Tans fellas got them within range, it might have had a more tragic ending. As it was, two of their number were captured, put on trial, and given three years penal servitude each. But they did not serve their full terms; when the treaty came they were released. One of them, Jim Kilroy, never looked back from that time forth; he went on to become a TD in the Dáil, and was hailed as a mighty freedom fighter. Poor Jim, really a genial easy-going man, did not do that much fighting, but that was the image of him that was built up for the people. The other, Daniel Dixon, joined the Guards at their inception but shortly afterwards got into bad health and died a young man.

Several times, my father with his friend and next door neighbour Henry Dixon, cousin to the man who was jailed, took men on the run across the bay by night in a boat, the same boat him and old Tom took the calves from the island in many years later. When he was well over seventy the Irish Government granted him a pension. It was not much but it was a help along with the old age pension. He was one of the last around our area to get the so-called IRA pension. Others who had done no more than he had in the troubles were drawing it for fourty years before he got it. As with many another thing it was not what you did that counted most: it was who you knew and how good a party man you were. You had to keep in with the right crowd and have the pull, and without that you might as well not expect much. It was always like that in Ireland and I'm afraid it's that way yet.

My mother's maiden name was Bridget Murray, but I never heard her called "Bridget" until her old age. She had to get the pension before that honour was bestowed upon her. For all her life before she was known as "Biddy". She was a straightforward woman. She said and did what she thought was right. She spoke her mind and acted on her initiative, and if people did not like it, well that was just too bad. It did not worry her.

And she was forever knitting. She knitted sweaters, and socks, and cushion covers, and many other things. She knitted when there was no need to knit because she liked knitting. Often I wished she would throw the needles away, but she hardly ever left them out of her hands, or so it seemed to me at the time. Later on, when she got old, I noticed that she had given it up: she had to, I believe, due to a combination of failing eyesight and the painful arthritis in the finger joints, which I have inherited from her. Though she was married young, at the age of twenty-one, she never had any children of her

56

own, except me. I was that rare bird in the locality, an only child, and I had to endure plenty of teasing on account of it, as if it was any fault of mine.

But my mother was not deterred. She wanted more children and if she could not have them herself, she could adopt or foster them. And she did. She took into her home and reared as her own three homeless children, three girls, Mary Jo, Eileen and Teresa. And she was every bit as good to them as she was to me, if not more so, because she felt they needed love and care more than I did. They had nobody else. "I gave them a mother's love", she said to me on her death bed. She did that, and they knew it, and they appreciated it. In their turn they were as good to her if not better than her own son was. They loved her very much.

CHAPTER SEVEN

Emigration or Dole

THE TIDE OF EMIGRATION, which had been draining the people away
ever since the time of the Great Famine, flowed strong in Erris where
I grew up. The most significant change in my time compared to
earlier times was that they no longer went to America. Emigration to
the United States had ceased in the early thirties and was not resumed
again until after the War. It was to Britain they went; there was not
much choice for them; they had to go somewhere, and bad and all as
Britain was in the pre-war years, and it was bad, there was less to be
got at home. Large families were the order of the day, nine or ten the
norm, and only one of them could remain on the land. The others had
to go. Very few found employment of any good in Ireland. For most
it was the emigrant ship, across the Irish Sea.

Many of the small farmers and their sons emigrated on a seasonal
basis, working on farms in the north and midlands of England during
the summer and autumn months and returning home in winter. Good
money was to be made at the beet in Yorkshire, Lincoln, and other
adjacent shires, but it was hard work, exclusively male, and not every
man was fit enough for it. Others went to Scotland to work at the
potato harvest, men, women and children—the tattie hokers they
were known as, but they were not in the same league as the beet men.
The beet workers could be described as the elite of the Irish migratory
agricultural workers. But there was nothing glamorous about their
work. It involved long arduous hours on piece work in the fields,
often from dawn to dusk, and under the most primitive living
conditions. They slept in huts provided by the farmers and looked
after themselves with regards cooking, washing and so on. It was
rough.

When they came home at the end of the season wearing their new
suits they were the envy of the rest of us. They always had the new
suits. No man I knew ever came home from the beet wearing the
same suit that he went away in. And those suits must have been mass

produced as so many of them were of the same pattern. One year they all came home with green suits; other years it was blue pin-stripes or checks, almost all identical. You might not know a man's name, or what townland he was from if you saw him walking along the street in Belmullet, or coming in to the dance hall, but one thing about him was easy to know—if he had been in England at the beet. That could be known right away from the suit he had on.

I had no hope of getting a new suit. I had to content myself with what I had and with dreaming of the day when I too would go away and come back at the end of the year with a brand new suit, a flashy shirt and tie, and a pair of red shoes. Meantime, I had to make do with the second-hand grey suit my mother had bought for me for thirty shillings from the Crossmolina man, Corcoran, who sold worn clothes on the street in Belmullet on fairdays.

In my experience emigration caused no great bitterness in the people's minds. It was accepted as a fact of life and it was both a curse and a blessing; on the one hand it drained the country of its youth; on the other, it provided an outlet without which I just do not know what would have happened. I remember in 1939, just before the outbreak of the War, the priest speaking in Borhauve Chapel advising young men to attend woodwork classes in the new technical school in Belmullet. "A joiner is a good job in England now", he said. "Joiners are earning up to seven pounds a week over there now." Wasn't that ironic! The priest on the altar telling people they should go to the technical school so they could train for working in England. And also, it gives an idea of what was considered excellent wages at the time. Seven pounds a week!

The politicians, as has always been the way of their kind, gave lip-service and platitudes no end to "the curse and the cancer of emigration". They were particularly vocal on this issue at election times, more so if they were for the opposition party. "The Government should do something", they would say, "to keep our people at home, by providing work for them here in their own country, at a decent living wage."

Like everything else, you could meet the political man who was an exception to that. I recall hearing one well-known and much-respected Erris man, who served for years as a member of the Dáil and as a County Councillor and ended up as a Senator, addressing an election meeting outside our chapel gate in the nineteen-forties, and saying he thought it was a good thing that people could go over to

England, earn good money there and come back again without any danger of them being drafted into the British Army, "thanks to our good wise Government who through negotiations with the British have made that possible".

A few young men from around our parts joined the Irish Army for the duration of the "Emergency"—the War. This was looked upon by most people I know as a complete waste of time for any right-thinking, able-bodied man. The pay was rotten, all they got for their soldiering was a token payment of a few shillings a week. That may have been all right for some of the town men, the kind of fellow who could be seen every day of the year holding up street corners, no good for anything, but not for country lads—good able workmen, who the people used to say, should go to some place where they could earn a few pounds. Some, after joining up, got fed up and deserted, and came home again. Whenever that happened the Guards came after them and arrested them and they were taken back to their units. And then it was the glasshouse for them.

At the labour exchange, better known as the dole office, they concentrated not so much on recruiting men for the Army as for the turf production scheme in the midlands. They could not make any man go against his will, nor take the dole off him for refusing to go, but they could make a damn determined effort to talk a man into going. A man from up the country came to the office a few times for that purpose—trying to procure peat workers, or as we knew them, turf workers. He would sound out several of the men who came in to sign on, yet with all his perseverance he was not able to wear down many of the Erris men. One lad from our townland went. Inside a fortnight he was back again, disillusioned. Then some funny joker put the rumour out that he had come to buy forty donkeys (asses) for putting out the turf off the bogs, and he did not like that one bit when he heard it. They gave him no more dole for the rest of that year. And that finished him with the Bog of Allen.

I applied for the dole as soon as I was eighteen. This involved undergoing a means test carried out by the pension officer. Only it wasn't my means that were tested but my father's. I had no means to test so they tested his instead. The day came when this very important person arrived driving a big black car, any kind of car was rare at the time, with the war-time shortage of petrol and all that. But that did not seem to have affected him. He was a small man in a tweed jacket and with black beady eyes, and they got blacker when he did not believe what we told him. By the time he left they were as black as the ace of spades.

My mother and I were in the house when he showed up; my father was out working with the pony and cart on the repairing of the road for the Board of Works. The first question he asked was where my father was, whatever that had to do with him; it was me that was looking for the dole, not my father. "Working on the road", we told him. "How much was he earning?" We told him that too. Six shillings a day I think it was. He marked the answer down in his book. My father being temporarily in paid employment did not mean much as far as the economics of the household were concerned; the job was only to last for a few weeks, but in our awe we forgot to point that out. He very probably knew it anyhow, all those old bog road repair jobs were much the same—a few weeks slavery in wintertime.

Then he wanted to know how many cattle we had and if we had sold any beasts within the past year. We told him we had two cows and a calf and that we had sold none. This was not true; we had sold a calf the summer before, but we were not so silly as to go telling him that, because then he would want to know how much money we got for her so that he could mark it down as income. My mother was doing most of the answering.

"Are the cows springers (pregnant cows), milk cows or dry cattle?"

"One springer, one milker and one calf."

"What age is the calf?"

"Over a year old."

This last reply prompted an argument, the inquisitor insisting that an animal over a year old was no longer a calf. It should be described as a heifer or a bullock, depending on whether it was a male or a female, he said. According to him, and maybe he had a point there, we wanted to make it look as if our animal was of less than its real value.

On his way into the house some hens which had gathered on the doorstep waiting to be fed had flown up wildly in his face, as hens will do when disturbed. They had regrouped and were making a cackling noise, wondering what was delaying their dinner. He asked my mother how many of them did she have and if they were laying. She told him she had about a dozen and that hens did not lay many eggs at that time of year. It was then the middle of winter, never a good time for hens laying, though some of ours still laid the occasional egg. In front of us on the dresser was a bowl and in it were some eggs she had been saving up to sell at the shopping lorry when it came round, to buy an ounce of tobacco for my father. It would be over a fortnight before his pay for working on the road came through and he suffered hell when the want of the tobacco was on him. The pension officer's sharp beady black eyes espied the eggs in the bowl and he demanded to know where they came from if the hens were not laying. "I didn't say they weren't laying. I only said they didn't lay many eggs at this time of year", replied my mother.

That was a true answer and it should have satisfied him, but he did not believe her. Many a time afterwards when I was thinking about it I wished I had suggested that he should round up the hens and try them like the country women used to do to find out if they were laying. "How can you expect me to do anything for you when you will not tell me the truth?", said the pension officer as he put his papers back into his briefcase. And if he said that once he must have said it about six times. He was sure we had told him nothing but lies. We might not have told him the whole truth, but we did not tell him that many lies. Very seldom did the pension officer get told all the truth.

Some weeks later I received a letter, postage paid by the government, to inform me that I had been granted the sum of four shillings unemployment benefit weekly, and should there be any change in my circumstances I was to let my local Exchange know at once, and so on. So that was that, I had the dole. My uncle Pat said that I was one of the lucky ones. Most of the young fellows got three shillings and one lad I knew was put out on two shillings a week. I had not fared too badly.

We were required to attend the dole office twice weekly: on Tuesday to sign on, which also involved a visit to the Guards Barracks for one of them to sign the form, and on Thursday to get paid. The office was a busy institution, with an all male clientage; women married or single must have been regarded as non-persons by the Government of the day, because they did not qualify for benefit. The only women ever I saw in the Belmullet Labour Exchange were a couple of young clerks who worked behind the counter. Their weekly wage was ten shillings, so they had more than their good looks to be snooty about. Familiarities were definitely not encouraged, as they regarded themselves to be well above the likes of us.

It took me a few months on the dole to save the two pounds I paid Sylvie Sweeney for a second-hand Raleigh bicycle, and then I was as good as the next man, I had my own bike, thereby having achieved one of my first great ambitions in life.

During the War we experienced shortages of many things in Ireland. Flour for baking was a problem to get and often we had to do with the boxty bread made entirely from potatoes. Boxty was a novelty at first but easy to get fed up with. When we did manage to obtain flour it was of a poor quality, "black flour" the people called it and it did not make nice bread. Tea was strictly rationed to half an ounce per week per person but could be bought on the black market for an exhorbitant price, smuggled in from the north. Geoffrey Hurst of Belmullet was an accomplished man for selling tea and other goods black market, as was John Doherty, the publican. Doherty kept the cigarettes and tobacco under the counter exclusively for good customers, meaning free spenders on the drink.

Paraffin oil for the lamps could not be got for love or money, black market or any other way and so we were all like the foolish virgins in the parable, we had no oil in our lamps. That was when the bog-deal came in useful. Many a time I read the *Irish Press* by the light of it at night for the old men who gathered visiting in Anthony Walsh's house. Well I remember reading for them Hitler's rantings about the new Europe he was going to build after the War was over, won by Germany and her allies. He was to find out different in the course of time.

Cattle prices had been pathetically poor all through the nineteen-thirties, the time of the economic war, but the outbreak of world war raised the farmers' hopes. In the 1914-18 War cattle prices had rocketed sky-high and everyone thought the same was going to happen again. Now they would get a splendid price for their beasts, they thought. But they were disappointed. "This is not a good war", said old Johnny Connolly. "The other war was a good war, but this one is hopeless!"

As the war continued the people kept up hopes that prices would eventually soar. When someone mentioned that the Pope was trying to arrange a peace: "I wish the Pope would mind his own business", commented an old friend and near kinsman of mine, a dealer who in anticipation of a price boom had stocked up with animals and now stood to gain or lose a small fortune. As it happened he lost and went out of the game.

In the early years of the war I admit to having had a passing regard for Hitler. It was not that I cared for the man or for anything he stood for. It was more to do with the fact that he was able for England. It was a bit like the day the school bully got his trouncing. England would not leave Ireland alone, but had been oppressing her for centuries and now it looked as if at last she had come up against her match. She was getting her own back now and although the guy who was giving her the hiding might not be a very nice fellow, he was knocking the hell out of the traditional enemy, and that was something. As time went by I changed my mind. Plenty of others, I am sure, felt the same way about it as I did, though they might not admit to it later on.

It was around that time I joined the Local Defence Force, a body of volunteers who were formed for the purpose of defending the country locally in the event of foreign invasion. They were a kind of civilian arm of the regular army. On enlisting we were obliged to take an oath. We swore to Almighty God that while we were soldiers and in the ranks of men (no women amongst us), we would be faithful to Ireland and loyal to the constitution, that we would obey all orders from our superior officers, and that we would not become members of, nor contribute to any illegal organisation. By this last clause was meant primarily the IRA which then, like before and since, was a thorn in the flesh of the established government, who kept hunting down its members and putting them out of the way, some for good. But no matter how many of its members were put out of the way the IRA would not go away, they had a way of bouncing back.

Training of our local company took place one night weekly in Shanahee old school under the tuition of Patrick Lavelle, who was the schoolmaster there by day. He had gone away somewhere for a fortnight at the holiday time to some army camp up the country to learn the rudiments of drill, etc., and he done his best to transmit what he knew into us.

Each man was issued with a green uniform, comprising of tunic trousers and overcoat, cap and badge, red boots and short red leggings. All this rig-out for free was an incentive for encouraging men and lads to join. The only difference between our uniforms and those of the regular army was that their uniforms had brass buttons, ours were of horn. And, but for the odd lapse, like the evening someone showed up for parade with his leggings on upside down, we were a smartly-turned out body of men at first, when the uniforms were new. But that did not last long, as they soon became the worst for wear, not through any fault of the material, but from over-use. The company was allocated a few rifles, given into the safe keeping of certain men: with each rifle went a limited number of bullets. Some fired theirs at birds and got into hot water for it. As lieutenant cum schoolmaster Lavelle said: "they were not handed out for shooting crows". They were meant for shooting men if need be, though I for one never thought about it in that way. I was confident that I would never have to do it, and if I thought I would I do not think I would have joined.

Rules governing the wearing of uniforms were seldom if ever obeyed. Officially we were to wear them at drill or parade meetings; as a concession they could be worn to Mass, provided a meeting or parade was to be held after Mass. But they were worn to places connected with neither Mass nor meeting. They were worn dancing and courting and doing many other things. By some they were worn full-time while they lasted. Any member leaving the country was supposed to hand his uniform in at the depot in Belmullet—but that was not always done either. I did not hand in mine and nobody ever came to collect it. It was there in the house for years. I don't know what became of it in the end.

CHAPTER EIGHT

Winkles and Oysters

PICKING WINKLES AND OYSTERS in the shores and out on the green beds when the tide was out was one slavish time and yet I enjoyed it. The shore was a cruel place to work in at any time, be it gathering manure or shellfish; and picking the winkles was the worst of all, and for little money. We picked them for four shillings a hundredweight, but before the war they were only going half that. It was in wintertime they were in season and that made it all the harder for us, as we laboured in the cold, bleak shores, turning over the stones and the sea wrack, searching for the little winkles. It was perishing cold on the hands, sore on the back, and hard on the eyes, and manys the winkle you picked before you had the full of the bucket never mind a hundredweight (about five average bucketfuls). A man named O'Malley from about Westport came around every few weeks in his lorry to buy them from us. O'Malley was a nice enough man but there was another fellow, John Joe Gallagher, who operated as a shellfish merchant at the same time. I sold winkles to him just once and I did not find him satisfactory. The man is dead and gone now.

Constant picking by several families made the winkles scarce in the shores near at hand and then the more ambitious of us moved further afield. In the two winters between the end of the war, when the market opened up again, and 1947, when I went to Scotland, I picked winkles along the western shore of Broadhaven Bay from Morahan ferry out to Ballyglass lighthouse, a distance of about nine miles. And I carried each day's picking back with me, in a bag on my back, around the winding shore, and with the water running out of them down into my wellingtons. Others did the same, and all for four shillings a hundredweight. And we had to keep them in bags in the sea-water until the man came to buy them, otherwise they would have died.

Oysters could only be found when the tide was far out. They were a more lucrative business than winkles, but harder to get at. Unlike now, no licence was required for fishing oysters at that time. We never dredged for the oysters like they do now, we just went out at low water and picked them up from the strand. When the spring tides came the water receded for miles in some places and then we were able to go out to where the oysters were. But we had to be always on the alert, we had to watch for when the tide started to come in, because when it did, it came fast, filling channels all around about everywhere. The unwary could easily get marooned out there. One needed to know the ground and to know the tide's movements, and to respect them, for if you didn't you might find yourself surrounded by water, and then it was God help you. A boat would be of little help, even if there was one around the place, which there was not. The sands became so soft at flow tide that the man stepping out of a boat to help a sinking man would himself go down. The sands could literally suck a person down so that he would never be seen again.

Only a few people ever ventured out on foot to the far oyster beds in Broadhaven Bay. They were Pat Walsh the blacksmith, and young Paddy Gaughan, better known as Paddy Pack, who was a young boy at the time, and my father and myself. Paddy was a lightweight and so he was able to walk on sands where the rest of us would sink. My father was a hardy man, a far hardier man than ever I was, and he was a good man to have with you on the strands; he was a careful man. As soon as the tide turned he would be calling on us to hurry towards the shore. Looking back on it now it's a wonder none of us got drowned. What stood for us was that we knew the strands like the back of our hands, we knew the good places and the bad places; we knew where we could walk with relative safety and we knew the treacherous parts which would engulf us if we set foot on them; I went very near getting lost one day and all because I stayed out too long for the sake of a few more oysters, until the strand got so soft I lost both my wellingtons, first one and then the other. But they were small loss, I saved myself. I jettisoned the bag of oysters, and by putting my weight on the bucket in front of me I kept myself from sinking, pulling myself along on all fours before the oncoming tide. That was how I made my way to the shore.

Three shillings a dozen was the price we got for the oysters in the mid forties; every time you picked one up it was as good as thruppence in your pocket. The agents in Belmullet who bought them from us were: first, John Doherty, and later, Jim Geraghty. They would not accept small oysters, anything under three inches in diameter was too small, and so they were not picked. They were out of season from May to August inclusive, any month without an "r" in its spelling was no good for oysters.

Only about once a year did we ever find scallops. That was about the middle of March, on the big "St Patrick's Day Strand" as it was locally known. The tide went out further then than at any other time during the year and only then were we able to get to the scallops off Shanahee Point. They were considered a great delicacy and we had no trouble selling them to the shopkeepers in the town for sixpence each. I believe they used to send them as presents to friends up the country.

Pat Walsh bought a curragh for shell fishing—a derelict old relic that he got for a few pounds from the Lally's of Ballyglass. He took it home by road on the cart; it couldn't be put on the sea because there were holes in it. After a lot of patching with canvas and tarring, lasting for several weeks, we decided to take it for a run to find out if it was watertight. Pat's wife, Molly, came with us as did young Paddy Gaughan. Pat and myself were rowing. I had never sat in a curragh before, never mind rowing in one. I knocked the skin off my knuckles with the paddles because I did not know how to use them. We called the oars of a curragh "paddles" and we called rowing in a curragh "pulling". And pulling in a curragh is easier talked about than done, especially when you don't know how. I just could not get the knack of it, not that first time anyhow. The damn fractious thing kept acting as if it had a mind of its own, kept turning around as if it wanted to go back again to the shore. Pat kept telling me to "pull even"—keep the same pressure on both hands and not to be bringing the curragh around in half circles on him; the people on the shore were watching, he reminded me and they would be laughing about us. "For Christ's sake will you try and keep the damn thing half straight." But it was no use. No matter how I tried the curragh would not go on a straight course or anything like it. When we had done a bee-line out for a few hundred yards offshore, we noticed a lot of bubbles boiling up from the bottom, out of the sea around us and we wondered what it was might be causing them. I said jokingly that maybe there was a submarine down there under us. That was shortly after the end of the War and it was rumoured there were still German submarines at large, lurking about in the seas. When Molly heard mention of submarines she nearly panicked, she thought we were going to be torpedoed. She did not do much complaining about my bad rowing when the curragh turned round again and this time we made for land. Of course there was no submarine there, the place was not deep enough for a submarine; what we had seen was something to do with the ebb or flow of the tide.

My father came with us the next time we went out. He was good in a curragh but on no account would he let me row and Pat Walsh gladly seconded him in that. They said I did not know how to row, which was true, but how can a person ever do anything if he is not given the chance to learn! From that day to this I have never rowed in a boat or a curragh. The curragh was too heavy from all the patching we had put on it, my father said; the lighter a curragh was, he claimed, the better; a heavy old tub was in danger of swamping. That curragh would have swamped sooner if it hadn't been patched. As it was, there was never much use got out of it. I think, like my grandfather's boat, it ended its days as a makeshift hen-house.

Pat Walsh and my father are gone now and so too is the oyster picking. Not a single oyster, I am told, can now be found in the Morahan strands. Times have changed and people have changed. The old people and the old ways have gone, and though it is possible to go there again and to walk once more in the old places, it can never be the same. In a sense there is no going back, we can never go back to what we left. If I may adapt the words of the Scottish song:

Those days are past now, and in the past they must remain,
we shall not see their like again.

We can never bring back the past.

CHAPTER NINE

The Long Road to Whithorn

IT WAS IN THE SUMMER of 1947 that I went to Scotland with the tattie squad. I was ready to go in 1946 but a week before I was due to leave I got struck down with a burst appendix. I was rushed to Castlebar Hospital, sixty miles away, in the middle of the night. My father gave seven pounds to John Doherty's son, Frank, for taking me to Castlebar in his hackney car that night, and seven pounds was money that was hard to find in those days.

They operated on me next morning and for three weeks I was kept propped up in bed almost in a sitting position. That was to give the drainer, which they had inserted into me, the benefit of gravity, so as to let the pus that was coming out of me seep into it. It was a rubber tube they had sticking out of my side and every day the nurse cut a piece of it off and threw it away and then she pulled it out a bit further until the whole tube was used. They were rough in those days, although they considered themselves far advanced, and I suppose they were, compared to former times when there would have been no hope for me.

I came home with the wound still running and with orders to attend the Belmullet District Hospital twice every week to have it dressed. When Dr Conway saw it he kept me there, in bed. His idea was that I should lie there, as still as I possibly could, in order to give the operation wound a chance to heal. Only in that way would it "consolidate", he said. But it did not consolidate.

I got a bad cold in there and a severe cough along with it which did not help my sore side, with its open wound. At the end of a fortnight I signed myself out and went home. The cold cleared up but the side did not heal. It kept running for about three months, until the piece of thread, about two inches long, which the Castlebar people had left inside me worked its way out of its own accord through the hole in my side. That happened, I believe, with the help of prayer (my mother was doing novenas galore for me). It did not take long in healing then. I missed going to Scotland that year but I was determined I would go the next year. And I did.

It was easy getting away with the tattie squads. They would take almost anybody, young or old, as long as they were able to pick potatoes. As Gruddy the ganger said, "all a person needed for the job was a good back and a willing pair of hands". The wages were four pounds a week for men (I don't remember now what it was for women and children) and your way was paid once you left the house until you arrived in the bothy.

On a lovely June morning three buses left Belmullet Square at ten o'clock and those three buses were full of men, women, adolescents and children—all bound for the potato fields of Scotland. For weeks previous the tattie gangers had been scouting around Erris looking for workers, and as anyone could see their efforts had borne fruit. The big and the small, the young and the old travelled that day; children who should have been at school and people bordering on the old age pension, the veteran who had walked the forty miles to Ballina the first time he went, half a century before, and the greenhorn setting out for the first time, who knew not what lay beyond Glen-castle or what he was letting himself in for. There were even in our company two tinkers, a young pair who kept aloof and who, I believe, regarded the rest of us with about as much distrust as we regarded them. In Ireland they had lived all their young lives with rejection and suspicion, and now they were going to try their luck in Scotland. I wondered if they were married. Charlie Keane said: "They'll just jump across the anvil when they get as far as Gretney Green."

The men who had assembled this collection of humanity were the tattie gangers—charge hands employed by Scottish potato mer-chants. They always came about the end of May every year, often accompanied by their wives. And it was not unknown for the ganger's wife to be more of a ganger than the ganger himself, wearing the trousers, a bit of a boss. Generally speaking, the gangers were not a bad bunch of men. They were usually local men who had first left home when they were very young; most of them had stuck with the same firm of merchants all their working days. Starting off as young hokers of potatoes they had in the course of time become charge hands. They had grown up and married, and matured, or become crabbit and contrary under the same bosses or their descendants. They had their foibles and their dodges, but as the fella said to me once about priests drinking: "Aren't we all human?"

To say their way of life was rough was not the half of it. It was primitive. The conditions they worked and lived under were shocking and the pay was nothing to brag about. But the job had its compensations. Some operated a nicely-paying sideline by selling the merchants' potatoes on the sly; others took advantage of the system by which the workers were paid (in loose cash) and cheated them. Some did both. A few got too greedy, got found out, and sacked; one or two went to prison. Most got away with it. And there were some who never worked any of the fiddles and in consequence never made much out of it.

One of the perks of the job was coming over annually to gather the squad, all expenses paid. Wearing a navy blue suit and a hat, a ganger could cut an impressive figure and was able to give a rosy account of what life was like in his particular squad. "Iron beds, flush lavatories and hot and cold water in our bothies." Most people knew that that was only talk, but as I said before, there was not much to be got at home.

Sometimes whole families, tired of struggling for an existence on the bit of half barren land and the few shillings a week dole, closed up house altogether and went away to Scotland with the tattie ganger; hence the presence of some very small children amongst the migrants on that day and on many a day as well as it. The intention was nearly always to come back home again in winter. Some came back, some never returned but made new homes across the water. Their hearths in Ireland remained cold and empty, and in time the homesteads fell into decay.

Three bus loads of people, with bag and baggage were assembled at the take-off point in Belmullet on that Thursday morning in June 1947, and one man in his hackney car had collected them, every one of them. To collect over two hundred people from the far flung corners of the barony was not an easy task for a man in his car to undertake, but Sonny Henaghan took it on, and he accomplished it. He did it all by himself and without any of the gains from it going to anybody else, because that was how he wanted it. He took on the job and he delivered the goods.

Henaghan had a plan and like all good plans it was a simple one. It meant starting to collect his passengers good and early—the day before to be to exact. It also involved telling lies to them. He came down to Morahan for Sonny Mack, Sonny Ritchie and myself at eight o'clock on Wednesday evening urging us to hurry and come with him as the time for the buses leaving had been changed. The buses, he told us, were leaving at ten o'clock that night, not ten next morning. So we got our few things together and away we went with him. He dropped us off on the square and went away for others. And that was how it went on all night, Henaghan collecting people and telling them the buses were leaving at different times. He changed the times to suit himself. We were there in the town all night, but no bus showed up, only Henaghan's car, full of people and luggage every time. We did not take it with good grace, but what could we do short of going home again. He had a patch on one of his eyes before the night was out. Someone had done something about it.

Morning came, five o'clock, six, seven, eight, nine, and a long drawn out summer's morning it was. At long last, at ten o'clock, the buses arrived and soon after that we were on our way, on the road to Dublin. And for all that day I had a raging headache.

Long before we reached Dublin most of us were completely flagged out. Yet there were amongst us a few gallant spirits who just would not give in. Kerrigan from Sraigh played a few tunes on his accordion, somebody else sang a song. It was a sad song that I often heard before and have often heard since about a young Irish girl who lost her health in America and came home to die.

> So fair youths and gentle maidens,
> Ponder well before you go,
> From your humble homes in Ireland,
> What's beyond you never know.

Whoever wrote that song wrote the truth. Some dropped off to sleep, but a certain Martin Geraghty slept none; he kept on and on, talking and jibing and telling smutty jokes. He was just like as if he had been wound up and maybe in a sense he was. I would have excused his blarney, but there was no stopping him, like the bus he just went on and on. Somewhere near Dublin Thomas Barrett asked me if I thought a hill which could be seen in the distance might be the hill of Tara where the kings of Ireland had their royal residence in ancient times. I did not know. I know now that it was not.

It was late afternoon by the time we reached Dublin. During the past twenty-four hours some of us had got our first taste of the exploitation that was to be our lot in the months and in the years to come. At Aston Quay several tough-looking middle-aged women

73

were conspicuous on the pavement, each with an alert and expectant air about her, and all looking much the same—no feminine attractiveness, untidy hair, hard grey faces and rough grey clothes. They were the bed and breakfast ladies from around Westland Row, and they were there looking for business. With two hundred passengers coming off our three buses, and all going to stay the night in Dublin, they had hit the jackpot. In a case like that one would think they could afford to take things easy. But no, that was not their way. One of them tried to pull the suitcase out of my hand, as half-dazed and bewildered I stepped off the bus. "Bed and Breakfast, come with me", said she. "Don't heed her, come with me", cut in another.

They were pushing each other and pulling and jostling us. Only for the ganger I don't know what we would have done. All day he had sat near to the front of the bus, him and another ganger, Nicholas Gallagher, and taken little or no interest in the rest of us. But now he had to take an interest if he wanted to keep his flock together, and being a man who had seen it all many times before, he knew what to do. Calling on some of the women by name (he knew them from previous encounters) he asked in a loud voice how many of us could each of them take. Soon we were struggling our way along the crowded pavement, Gruddy and the women in front, and us following. If I was at home then I would have stayed at home, but one consolation at least, I knew I would not be spending a second night standing around on the street. Never before had I slept in a room with seven others. That night was my first time, but not my last.

Later that evening Charlie Keane and I walked along Westland Row and into Pearse Street. It was coming near the end of what had been a glorious fine summer's day. People hurried after their various pursuits, more people than I had ever seen before, and I remember thinking that I would not like to be in Dublin on my own. We went into a public house at a corner, where we each drank two bottles of Guinness and ate a packet of biscuits between us. And we needed them. Except for the cups of half cold tea and the ham sandwiches in Mullingar I had not seen or tasted any of the free grub we were promised. Then we went back to base and to bed.

I had no trouble in going to sleep that night or in finishing off the bacon and egg next morning, and I did not worry about it being Friday—a day of abstinence. Martin Keane said that if the bunch of flowers on the table were the real thing and not made of coloured paper he could have eaten them too, so hungry was he.

74

We crossed the Liffey to Amiens Street and it was there we got the Belfast train in transit for the Glasgow boat. It was my first time on a train and I cannot say that I remember much about it except that at one stage Martin Ruddy thought he had lost his suitcase and got excited about it, but it was all right, it was in the guard's van. The rest of us had our cases in the carriage with us. In Belfast we had another long period of sitting around, this time in the railway station, and then a trek from station to quay, still clutching our cases.

A smelly embarkation, lights twinkling along the coast as the boat moved out of the lough, intermittent flashes from a lighthouse, and a midnight snack at sea, our first breaking of bread since early morning, those snatches of recollections remain in my mind. So overcrowded was the boat that night that there was not a hope of everybody getting a seat, nor the chance of a place to lie down for a few hours. My suitcase, a hand-me-down from my uncle, and now long past its best, had been sat and trampled upon so often, and flung about so much, it was showing signs of giving way at the joinings. Were that to happen it would have been a calamity for me, as it held all my earthly goods. So placing it in a corner I sat myself down beside it. I slept briefly and awoke with the headache back again. This headache was becoming a nuisance and I had neither powder nor tablet to relieve its pain.

Dawn on Saturday morning saw us coming up the Clyde estuary, past Ailsa Craig, "Paddy's Milestone", a huge column of rock sticking up out of the sea. A young girl of our company said it was flung out there long ago by Fionn McCool, after some Scottish giant, who, having been beaten by Fionn in a fight in Northern Ireland (there must always have been trouble in that place) had taken to his heels and escaped by jumping across the sea to Scotland. The woman beside her said she did not believe a word of it. "It never happened, that rock was always there", she maintained.

I can remember of no drinking on the boat that night. Anyhow our crowd, even had their pockets allowed for it, were too tired and worn out to be bothered. Fatigue had got the better of them and for the most part they were listless and disinterested. But not all of them. Like on the bus to Dublin there were amongst us a few brave and resilient souls who were determined to go right on to the end of the road in good spirits, and, although I did not think about it at the time, their example must had been a help to the others. Margaret Carey was singing: "We are sailing away from the land we loved and the homes we loved with pride", and with her chin resting on her hand she gazed at the coast of Scotland. I had often heard her sing at the dances at home. After that morning I never saw her again. The man with the accordion, not to be outdone, struck up tune again in his own off and on spasmodic way. Nobody made any attempt to dance.

And so we came, slowly, slowly up the Clyde, past Greenock on one side, with its ships in the making, and Dumbarton with its big rock on the other side, past Clydebank with more ships and more big cranes, on up into a growing stench of smoke and soot and oil, right up to the Broomielaw. My first impressions of Glasgow were not good—long row after row of dismal-looking, smoke-blackened buildings. By the time we left the boat I was feeling within me an emptiness and a depression which I never had before, but which I was to come to know well in the months ahead.

It was there on the waterfront that, without ceremony, we parted company with all our friends from the other squads, who had been with us all the way from Belmullet. Some of them I have not seen from that day to this. Many have long since gone to their eternal rewards, or the way of all flesh, whichever way you want to put it. They were herded off that morning, some to catch the Edinburgh train, others away to Fife. For us it was another walk, to Queen Street, and another long wait outside the goods station until finally about midday, we boarded an open lorry, the property of the potato merchant, which would deliver us to our place of work—the Isle of Whithorn by the sea, on the southern tip of Scotland, one hundred and thirty miles by road from Glasgow. And thank Providence the weather still held. We would have been a sorry sight had it been raining. The ganger travelled in the cabin beside the driver.

First we passed through a maze of dark streets. People on the pavements stared at us. One of a group of young men standing at a corner shouted "Irish tattie howkers" after us. It was out Pollokshaws Road we went, and I remember thinking that it was an awful long street. For miles, or so it seemed to me, "Pollokshaws Road" was written on every corner. By Newton Mearns things had taken on an entirely different look. Now it was all big posh houses and luxurious-looking bungalows with lovely flower gardens. Soon we were in the open country, passing by green fields on either side of the road; lush fields in which grazed herds of black and white cattle, cattle with the biggest udders I had ever seen.

In the town of Girvan we were treated to Irn Bru and chips, the first time I had ever drunk Irn Bru or eaten potato chips. I was to get well used to them in the years that followed. Some of us, who had taken advantage of the delay to run up an alleyway in answer to nature's call, were reprimanded in a brusque but friendly manner by the driver: "Ye's are not in Ireland now. Ye's will go to jail if ye's are caught pissing there, so ye's will."

Past Girvan we could see faintly, away on the horizon to the south-west, the hill of Antrim. At Stranraer we turned left, and then we were on the last leg of our long and tiresome journey. It was a long road to Whithorn and the Isle lies three miles beyond it.

The Isle of Whithorn is not an island. It is a quiet seaside village consisting of little more than a crescent shaped line of houses fronting a small harbour, with the inevitable hotel, two pubs and a few shops. Part of the adjacent headland was a tiny island in days gone by, and that is how the place got its name; but it is now joined to the mainland, the narrow channel having been filled in by dumping ballast from boats into it about the middle of the last century, or so I was told by the locals. That headland is steeped in history, and has the remains of both a Viking settlement and an early Christian church. But these were matters about which we neither knew nor cared as bedraggled, exhausted and hungry, we halted at a farmstead near to the village on that sunny June Saturday afternoon so many years ago.

CHAPTER TEN

The Bothy

UNDER THE SYSTEM by which we worked, the merchant, based in Glasgow, bought the crops of potatoes from the farmers while they were still in the ground. The workers, employed by the merchant, lifted and gathered the crop which was then conveyed in the merchant's lorries to the nearest railway station. From there it was taken by rail to Glasgow to be distributed to various wholesalers and others. The workers thus engaged led, by necessity, an itinerant lifestyle, moving around from one farm to another. Finished in one place, they moved, lock, stock, and barrel, to the next. Living accommodation of a sort was provided for them on the farms; for the most part it was of a deplorable nature—in old nissen huts, in hay sheds, and in cowbyres. Any old place at all was good enough for the "tattie howkers". It was a rough life. Nobody seemed to worry about sanitation, and just as well they didn't, because it was non-existent. We had to make do as best we could, discharging our natural bodily functions under what cover we could find, such as along hedges and behind bushes. Apartheid of the sexes was generally dealt with by housing the men in one end of the byre and the women in the other, partitioned off by a large curtain made from empty potato sacks sewn together. Married couples were usually assigned quarters to themselves, but that is not to say they enjoyed much privacy, as more than one couple, sometimes several, often had to share the same department.

Our place by the Isle of Whithorn fitted the conventional. It was a large cow-house from which the four-footed animals had been recently ejected to make way for the Irish potato workers. Some half-hearted attempt had been made to give the place a bit of a face-lift, but the limewashing and the hosing out had not removed all traces of the former occupants. The empty stalls were still there, and so too in places was the hardened cowdung, sticking to the walls.

One of our first tasks after moving in was to set up beds for ourselves in two rows along the wall, a row on each side where the cows had been, a bed in each empty stall, with heads to the wall and feet towards the middle of the floor. Bedding material was already there in plenty awaiting us in the form of flat, empty potato-sprouting boxes for base, straw to fill into sacks for mattresses, and ex-army blankets—two blankets per person, all thoughtfully provided by the merchant.

Martin Keane and myself made ourselves a double bed. That was the general rule—two men to every bed. Martin had been there before and he knew the ropes. With double beds we had more blankets and could put one under us to ease the discomfort of lying on the coarse sacking. We were not supplied with pillows, a bag of straw served that purpose, and sheets were luxuries we had to do without. As for the blankets, they could have done with a wash, the Lord only knows how many people had slept under them, and they were mouldy along with that. But we had to accept them, there was nothing we could do.

Some of the women went to the village for vitals to tide us over the weekend, and came back with loaves and jam, and tea and sugar. Each person was asked to contribute towards the purchase expense, two shillings, I think, was what I paid. All paid up except two who said they would manage fine on the potatoes that were for free and the milk that could be bought on the farm for a few pence a pint. But before the weekend was out they were going around scrounging for mugs of tea.

Cooking was done over a charcoal fire outside in the open air. The fire was between two low brick walls and with a sheet of strong mesh wire laid across the top. It made a good enough hotplate in dry weather, but it was punishment trying to cook anything on it when it was raining.

By evening the place looked a lot better, especially the women's part. They had gone to a considerable amount of trouble trying to make it a bit civilised looking, a few had brought bedspreads and pillows with them from Ireland, even table-cloths, which they spread over wooden boxes. The three married couples, one of whom had two young children, had the exclusive use of the loft and each couple cordoned off a section for themselves, again with the potato sacks. Those empty bags were used for many purposes other than for holding potatoes. Not only were they useful and handy for bedding purposes, they were stuffed into holes in the walls to keep out the draughts and the rats, and out in the fields on wet days we wore them

79

over our heads and shoulders for protection against the rain. We cut them up and wound them around our legs like puttees for protection against the early morning dew, which saturated the potato fields and could soak a person to the skin in minutes, and the pickers who laboured on their knees in the wet stoney earth wore them around their lower limbs like the bandages of an Egyptian mummy. The empty bags played a useful role in the bothy life of a tattie hoker of the late nineteen-forties, and that I can say without hesitation. Even the women who stayed in to look after the bothy wore them as aprons.

Later that first evening we were visited by three people from Achill, two men and a woman, who worked and lived on a nearby farm. They had noted our arrival and decided to pay us a courtesy call. The woman's name was Mary Lavelle. One of the men was named Stafford, the other Kerby—strange names, I thought, but as I was to discover there are many surnames in Achill which sound strange to an Erris man. In the course of conversation the woman mentioned to me that they always got on "fairly good" with the Belmullet crowd. "But they have a way of their own", she remarked. I said I had often heard the Achill people had a way of their own too. She laughed at that and put the conversation no further. In the course of time I was to learn that people are much the same everywhere. The good and the bad are not confined to places, races or religions. Our Achill visitors went away and then we went to bed, but not all at the same time. Some of the older people turned in first. By midnight everybody was sleeping under the army blankets, on their beds of straw.

Sunday was a quiet day. It was a day of rest if not of worship for all of us. Some of the squad went to Mass in a town a few miles away, having first walked into the village and there hired a taxi. Of this I knew nothing at the time as I was still fast asleep when they left. Later on in the day some of us went on into the village. Soldiers were hanging around near a camp beside the road; they were watching us, but did not speak, did not reply even when we bade them the time of day. At home in Ireland everybody spoke to everybody else on the road. On reaching the village, two of our party, McAndrew and Geraghty, "monied men" as Charlie Keane called them, managed to get into the hotel for a drink. There they met the ganger, Gruddy, who with some others had gone in on their way back from Mass. They returned to the bothy late that evening, all in high spirits, and they had with them a new man, a dark skinned sort of gipsy fellow called

Hamilton, who had been working in the squad the previous year, and was now back; yet another to be installed in the cow byre.

Meantime, Martin Keane, Charlie Keane and myself walked along the seafront promenade. It was a fine day. We got talking to an oldish man who was standing, leaning on the wall, looking out to sea—a civil man. I asked him if some land that could be clearly seen out there was Ireland. "No", he said, "that is the Isle of Man, and see those hills further away to the left, that is part of England." He told us the villagers were on good terms with the tattie squads, and he was able to name most of the men who had been with Gruddy the year before. But from they way he talked I gathered that the soldiers were not so well liked. I remarked that they did not seem very friendly. "They will be friendly enough with the women, the randy buggars, if they get half the chance", he replied. He was right there. Those soldiers turned out to be a damn nuisance before long, prowling around the women's quarters at night. Maybe they got some encouragement too. It might not have been all their fault.

Back at the bothy I sat for a time on the grass down near the seashore. It was boring with no way to pass the time. At home there would be something to do on a Sunday evening, but this place was sickening, no radio, no music, no anything; the man with the accordion had parted from us in Glasgow. Before going to bed I wrote a letter to my people, a long letter of about four pages. I said I missed everybody and everything at home, and I asked about all the neighbours. I even asked about our own dog and pony. Then I must have thought it was a bit too poignant, because I tore it up and wrote a shorter and a more cheerful one instead, which I put into the mail box beside the road so as to be on its way first thing in the morning. I had to borrow the stamp from one of the others.

As I explained earlier on, we slept two to a bed in two rows of makeshift beds on either side of the byre. The newcomer, Hamilton, had no bed mate. He made up, or rather laid down a single bed for himself at the end, next to where myself and Martin Keane slept. That night after everybody had settled down and everything was quiet, Keane reached over and made a scratching noise with his fingers on the side of the wooden box which served as the new man's bed base. The fellow, when he heard this, jumped out of bed, clawed around in the dark for a box of matches he had somewhere near, and having found them he lit a candle, the only means of artificial light there was in the bothy. He then commenced to pull his bed apart.

"What the bloody hell is the matter with you over there?" shouted a man in one of the beds on the other side.

"There is an effing rat in my bed", came the excited answer.

"There is no rat in your bed, put out the light", he was told.

"I tell you there is a effing rat, didn't I hear the effer. This place was full of them last year and they're here again this year", shouted the new man.

"Shut up, you only imagined it", said another.

"Did I fuck imagine it", cried the bloke, pulling the straw out of the bags and beating it with one of his boots.

At last, satisfied the rat was gone, he put his bed back together, got into it again and put out the candle. Some minutes later Keane repeated the scratching.

"There is the fucker again", shouted Hamilton, more excited than ever. "I heard him again, chewing like fuck, the bastard", and he jumped out of bed again and lit the candle a second time.

Everybody was now wide awake, and some not very happy at having been roused from their sleep. Oaths and curses were flying. The young gipsy lad had as good if not a better collection of swear words as any man there and he did not spare using them. I, not having been used to hearing such foul language used so freely, thought the ground might open up at any minute and swallow us all down to the fellow with the horns. Keane, beside me, was puffing, trying to keep from laughing. I think in the end the guy suspected a trick was being played on him. Anyhow, he quietened down and soon afterwards I went to sleep. Before many weeks had passed we had rats in plenty and we had no need to invent them.

So passed my first Sunday in Scotland, and although I did not know it then, things would never be the same for me again. The ice was broken. I had started the process which was to sever me away from Ireland, and tie me to Scotland, where one day I would make my home.

CHAPTER ELEVEN

Tattie Hoking

IT WAS EARLY DAWN. I was awakened by an awful racket of shouting. You would think that all hell had broken loose; it was the ganger wakening us up. "Get up out of that ye lazy shower of greecians." "Greecians" was his way of pronouncing the slang term "greensheens", a Scottishism meaning the same as green horns—newly overs. "Get up ye big sleepy heads", he roared again. "Do ye's not know what time it is? Ye's have to be in the fucking field at six o'clock."

That was how he went on every morning, except that his language was even riper than I have quoted, as he came tearing through the place, pulling blankets off beds left and right, and yelling as if he had taken leave of his senses and the oaths and the obscenities came tumbling out. He had a few minutes of madness at the beginning of every working day and then he settled down and was a pleasant enough fellow. Oh! What would I not have given at that time of the morning for one more hour under the old army blankets and with the dried cow-dung on the wall behind my head.

All around men and boys were pulling themselves out of bed, rubbing the sleep from their eyes, and pulling on their trousers. And there was nothing for me but to do likewise, and hurry to the communal eating place (an adjoining shed) to gulp down the bread and jam and the tea from the galvanised urn.

Out in the fields we were allowed two tea breaks daily, the first at about nine o'clock in the morning and the second about noon, but not always at exactly the same time. That depended on when the two women who stayed in and looked after the bothy came out with it; it could vary half an hour or more either way some days. They would show up every fine day, they and the children, carrying the eternal bread and jam, and with mugs, and kettles of cold tea. The ganger, fair play to him, would nearly always have a fire going in the field when they came, made up of dry sods and sticks and twigs, to place the kettles on in order to warm up the tea again. He would have been doing that for his own sake as well as ours, but we appreciated it just the same. When the weather was nice it was quite enjoyable, sitting taking our tea out there in the fields. On wet days the women did not come out and then we rode into the bothy on the back of the tractor and took our tea there; but seldom was it so wet that we did not go out to work again.

It was up to ourselves if we wanted to boil potatoes in the evenings when the day's work was over. They could be had for free and there was no shortage of old tin cans and buckets to boil them in. For my part I could not be bothered boiling potatoes. In those days of meat rationing it was very hard to get anything to take with them and I never saw vegetables used while I was in the squad; I never had a right dinner while I was there. A man could put his weekly allowance of two ounces of bacon into his waistcoat pocket, and butcher meat was impossible to get. They just would not sell it to us—kept it for better customers. Butter too was tightly rationed—two ounces per week. That was why there was so much jam and margarine. My first week's ration of butter mysteriously disappeared from the bedside box the same evening as I got it. The following week I put it into my suitcase for safe-keeping, but the humid weather caused it to melt all over my one and only Sunday shirt. On the advice of some of the women, and with the help of an old smoothing iron that I got the loan of, I succeeded in getting most of the grease out of the shirt by ironing and re-ironing it under a sheet of brown paper. By then, I was fed up and far from home and sorry I ever bothered coming to the tattie hoking.

The work was hard, drudging and monotonous. Ten or twelve people toiled side by side in a row all day long, every day, digging potatoes, two drills at a time with short three pronged forks, known as "tattie graips". On the outside of the line was a sort of foreman digger—a leading hand, setting the pace. He was the guiding star of the squad. Without him we might have started striving to see who could dig the fastest, or we might slacken off and go slow, depending on what kind of humour some of us might be in. But that was not allowed, everyone was to take their cue from the leading digger, and no one was to go faster than him or to fall behind. In some squads the leading digger was a woman, and some of those women were good hands with the graip; they could show how it was done to any man.

The pickers followed after us as we dug, often on their knees when their back could stand it no longer, sacks bound around their legs as they gathered the potatoes into baskets. Small or damaged potatoes, "the broke" as they were called, were left on the ground to be collected later after the whole field had been dug. This was done by the whole squad, walking along in a line and picking as they went, every two holding a basket between them. As the baskets of good potatoes were being filled they were lifted and emptied into sacks by men who were called "timmers" because their job was timming or emptying the baskets. The sacks when full were sewn closed with a pack needle and then loaded on to the tractor by two other men, the loaders. The tractor took them to a makeshift platform by the roadside and from there they were transferred to the lorries. The ganger, graip in hand, would go scraping around looking for any good potatoes that might have been missed out. Whenever he found any he would fling them in the direction of the pickers' backsides with a warning to them to pay more attention to what they were doing.

We started work early in the mornings, usually at six o'clock and sometimes earlier. Whenever an urgent word came for more potatoes, as nearly always happened coming near to the end of the week, then we had to start very early, often at four o'clock in the morning, and keep going, through rain of shine, until the required amount was produced; then we got the rest of the day off. It was no job for sleepy heads or for anyone with a bad back, and most of the people who stuck with it for a number of years ended up with sore backs and rheumatism and other pains which they never got rid of.

After we were about a month around Whithorn a mechanical potato digger arrived (the only one the merchant had) and then most of the diggers were downgraded—they became pickers. The work progressed a lot faster, and a few like myself who were considered strong in the arm were moved up in rank to reinforce the timmers and the loaders.

Our evenings after finishing work were spent hanging around the bothy or going for walks into the village, or up to the other bothy where the Achill people were. Some of the fellows played pitch and toss with pennies on the road. More often I spent the evenings lying on my bed, so tired I was after been up since before the break of day. Several times I slept right through to the morning without taking off my clothes or going to bed properly.

The Rhinns of Galloway, where we moved to after leaving the Whithorn area, is green and pleasant, an island like place with sandy beaches in some places and rocky cliffs in other parts around its shores; it is almost entirely surrounded by water. Looked at from the map or from the air it has the shape of a huge shoe sticking out into the sea. Its land is rich and fertile, ideal potato-growing country, and it has a grand view from its high points. The hills of Northern Ireland are clearly visible on a clear day and one can follow the line of the road along the Antrim coast and see the houses. I used to stand on a high place beside some tower or monument and look longingly across the blue hills. It might be the north, the so-called black north over there, but it was Ireland just the same, and I loved to look over at it.

Kirkholm, the village we worked beside in late August, is a quiet place along the Carsewall road. It had two pubs in my time, one at each end of the village, and it was said to have had at one time, a minister who was a very eloquent and dedicated preacher. He was so wrapped up in it all that even after his death he would not rest in peace—his ghost kept coming back to interrupt the new man's sermons. Finally he was exorcized by the new Minister, a Reverend MacGregor, and his last words were, "Roar awa MacGregor, I can roar nay mair", meaning in plain English, roar away MacGregor, I can roar no more. Silenced, and banished from the church into a nearby lake, he still haunted the place for many years. He would grab anybody bold enough to venture that way after dark and try to dip them into the lake. When he lived he had always been a great believer in baptism by immersion. That story did not go far into my head.

Several other tattie squads besides ours worked within the Rhinns Peninsula at that time. A man named John Barrett was in charge of about thirty workers, mostly youngsters from the Glosh and Faulmore district of Erris. There was also a squad under Andrew Lynskey from Belmullet, and another under a fellow they called "the spitfire", his right name has escaped my memory. An Achill squad worked under old Pat Toolis, a cranky old man who, considering the crowd he had to put up with, had plenty to be cranky about. And there were two Arranmore Donegal squads. All did not work for the same merchant.

We were housed in disused army huts. The area had been a military base during the war and though there were still soldiers around, many of their living quarters were now vacant. They were taken over for the squads and were a vast improvement from the cow-houses. The running water had been cut off, and the cooking and electrical facilities had also been removed, but some of the huts still had army iron bedsteads in them, a luxury to us after sleeping on potato boxes.

Some queer characters floated around there. One in particular, a Dublin man who worked in Lynskey's squad, was a deserter from both the British and the Irish armies. You would think that having found things so much to his dislike in one army that he ran away from it, he would not have joined another. But as the man said, he must have been a glutton for punishment—he joined and deserted both. It was an open secret about him, but nobody would dream of having him turned in, our minds did not work in that way. Being an army deserter he could not go looking for an identity card, and without an identity card he could not get a ration book, so that left him out on a limb. He was forever on the cadge, asking for one thing or another, and he was not above taking things without asking for them if he got the chance. All the clothes he had was an old grey suit, over which he pulled on overalls at his work and a pair of wellington boots. He had a pair of down at heel shoes for wearing in the evenings. According to those who slept in the same hut as him, he used to grind his teeth and curse and swear in his sleep. And the grinding of the teeth is a most annoying thing to have to suffer from anybody. Some years later, I slept for some time in the same bed as a man who did it, and believe me it was no joke to put up with.

Believe it or not, this man in the bothy had a girlfriend, a woman in the village whose husband had left her. Those were the days when sweets could not be bought without coupons, and as he had no ration book he had no coupons. He asked me one evening for some as he was going to the woman's house and he wanted to buy sweets for her children. I handed him my ration book, which had two leaves of confectionery coupons in it, and I said: "take a few out of that". I did not mind him having some as I was not particularly fond of sweets and usually gave away my coupons. I thought he would take maybe three of four, but what did the bloody man do but tear out a whole leaf, half of all the coupons I had. I grabbed hold of him and forcibly took them back. Then I gave him two coupons, enough to buy a quarter pound of sweets. And that was good enough and too good for him; he was lucky to get any at all.

He was a good dancer and used to go up to the old hall beside the back road, himself and the woman. She affectionately called him "Johnny", but I don't think that was his name. To us he was known as "the quare fella", and that was long before Brendan Behan's play of that name was ever heard of. And he was a queer fellow; any man could get a woman when he got one.

Late on the evening before I left there, I found him sitting outside one of the huts, shivering and almost in tears, with his lip cut and bleeding where one of the men had hit him, something to do with sexual advances he had allegedly made to the man's sister-in-law, a girl in her early teens. It must have been that one woman wasn't enough for him, he wanted a young bit. He had his problems.

So too did another, a youngish red-haired man who worked on a nearby farm and took to hanging about the bothies most evenings. The strange thing about this bloke was that he seemed to be far more interested sexually in the young lads than he was in the girls. This was something new to me, I had never come across a man like that before. I just did not know what to make of him, or how it was that he had his sexual priorities all wrong. I had never heard of the likes, neither had some of the others. One girl from Faulmore knew what he was. "He is a nancy boy, that's what he is", she said; "a good thrashing, that's what he needs". "What's a nancy boy?" someone asked. "A nancy boy is a man that does be going after other men. Can't be bothered with the women at all. There was one like that in Perth last year", she went on. "Dressed up in women's clothes some of the time, so he did. Oh, there is plenty of them in this country", she told us. Others, amid a lot of laughing agreed with what she was saying.

The long and the short of it was we decided to give the man a lesson. That evening when he came up, five or six of us set about him. He did not fight back, but ran. We chased after him. We were not able to catch up with him, so we let the stones fly. They were hopping off his back as he went down the lane and us after him. After that he did not come back near the place again.

Dances were held on Sunday nights and sometimes on week nights too, in an old hall along a side road. It was a strange place for a hall and I think it must have been an army place of some sort to begin with but at that time nobody seemed to have complete control over it. As far as I know when the youngsters felt like holding a dance they had a word with the man on whose land it stood—all they needed was his permission to dance there. I don't know whether he charged any money for the use of it or not. And they would dance there until midnight or after to the music of a fiddler from Achill. A cap was passed round until it had done the round of the hall and everybody put something into it for the fiddler. Lighting in the hall was from a tilly lamp that gave trouble. The only man able to get the lamp going right was "the quare fella". The dancing was enjoyable while it lasted but it was sheer hell getting up the following morning.

I do not recall ever seeing any soldiers at those dances and just as well, for we did not like them. But two Northern Ireland men, brothers by the names of George and Jimmy Plant, were regular attenders. Those two were forestry workers and they lived in a small hut amongst the trees on the other side of the village. We called them the woodcutters. George, the older of the two, offered me a job along with them. He told me they could do with a third man, mainly for cutting up and burning the rubbish. I would probably have been no worse off had I joined them. They nearly always had fires going around where they worked, you could see and smell the smoke for miles around, and they made a continual din with their power saws cutting up wood. Lorries came sometimes and took away loads of big logs from them. They were nice, civil men, but the work was hard and the life was a lonely one.

The last place I worked at was called Salchie Farm. From the fields beside the sea you could almost throw a penny on to the deck of the Stranraer-Belfast steamer, the "Princess Victoria", which was lost so tragically afterwards. Every morning she sailed out Lock Ryan and away to the south-west beyond the lighthouse on the point, making for Belfast. The Dublin boat too could be seen sometimes in the late evenings, making its way slowly down the Irish Sea. Often I wished I was on one of them. I hated the tattie hoking and was feeling depressed and miserable at times. But I was to get away from it sooner than I thought I would, and this is how it came to pass.

One Sunday evening, the ganger came over to where I was sitting on a grassy slope outside the bothy and a letter in his hand with him. I knew when I saw him coming that he had something on his mind, because he never took his letters to me to read, he was well able to do that for himself. I soon found out what it was, as he came to the point at once. How would I like to go in and work at the station in Glasgow for a while, he asked. He then proceeded to read the letter to me. It had been hand-delivered to him that day by one of the lorry drivers, he informed me. The gist of it was that they wanted a "good man" to help with loading and unloading at Queen Street Station and as he had several adult men in his squad they hoped he could provide one who was suitable. I was the second man he had offered the job to, he said. He had already asked his brother, but he did not want to leave the squad. "It's the woman", he remarked, alluding to the brother's girlfriend. "he does not want to leave her." "And it's no use asking them married fellows, they can't very well go. So what about you?"

It was a good chance, he said, whether he meant it or not. I was glad of any chance to get away from there. I was fed up to the teeth with the life and with the work and it did not require any persuasion to make me accept the offer. He wrote out and gave me a note for the merchant's foreman in the station and also the address. And I was to be sure and take it with me and not to lose it, he said. "Glasgow is a big place." I would get the red bus to Waterloo Street Station at nine o'clock tomorrow morning, he told me. He did not mention anything about fare.

Joe Gruddy then walked away and from that day to this I have never laid eyes on him. I do not know if he is living or dead. He was not a bad man according to his lights. It was easy to find worse. He had his moods and his dodges and his early morning mad fits of shouting, but he had his good points as well, more so than many a ganger I have worked under since.

As there was no need to get up with the others in the morning it was my intention to lie on in bed for a while, but not one wink of sleep could I get since before it got bright, nor content myself in bed, so excited I was at the prospect of going to stay in Glasgow. I had two uncles and an aunt living there, plus a number a cousins, and to be near them would be almost like being at home, I was thinking. So glad was I to put the place behind me I did not wait for the bus to come, but set off walking the eight miles into Stranraer. It was a fine morning, the case was not heavy, and it did not take me long to cover a bit of the road. I was nearing the town when the bus passed me by. Never again would I sleep in a potato bothy.

CHAPTER TWELVE

Queen Street Station

ABOUT THREE HOURS it took the bus from the time it left Stranraer until it pulled into the old station in Waterloo Street, Glasgow, good going considering all the stops we made along the way, not only in the towns but at any number of places along the road as well. Once or twice we passed close to where tattie squads worked in the fields, men and women, and children too, with the canvas sacks around them, picking away as fast as they could after the digger. By the time we reached the outskirts of Glasgow it had started to rain.

As I was leaving the bus I asked the conductor if he could tell me how to get to Florence Street. "Nae bother", he said. I was to turn left and go along Argyle Street until I reached Glassford Street, "three or fours streets along", and from there any number thirteen Cathcart tram would take me the rest of the way. "But mind and get off at Cumberland Street", he called after me. "Nae bother", the man had said, meaning it was no bother, and memorising his instructions was no bother to me. I had a marvellous memory in those days, and I can still remember things that happened then a lot more clearly than I can remember recent happenings. So off I went along Argyle Street. It being about lunchtime there was a big crush of people on the pavement, and all of them in a hurry. I had enough to do to keep them from knocking the case out of my hand in their haste as they sped along in the rain.

I found Glassford Street and took my place at the end of the queue beside the tram stop. I knew I was in the right place. The man had said it was a number thirteen car I should get, and sure enough thirteen was one of the numbers up on the post over the stop. I was not long waiting when a number thirteen came along, but with "Maryhill" on the front of it, not "Cathcart". The man had not said anything about Maryhill, only Cathcart. So that puzzled me and as I was not sure what to do I asked the woman in front of me if this tram would take me to Cumberland Street. "Ye'll never get a caur tae

Cumberland Street on this side", said she, giving me a look as if I was daft. "Can ye no see it's gaun the wrang way." And with that she stepped on to the tram and I was left standing there, myself and my old suitcase, in everybody's way, looking like a fool. "Away over to that stop on the other side of the road, son", said a man beside me, "You'll get the car you want over there."

In response to this information I crossed the street to where several trams were lined up, nose to tail, and having squeezed my way between them, on to the pavement, I saw that one of them was what I wanted, a "13 Cathcart". So I clambered aboard with my suitcase. I still must have been unsure of myself because I asked the man in the seat beside me if this car passed by Cumberland Street, and he said: "It crosses Cumberland Street." We moved off and between the stopping and the starting we were soon across the Clyde and nobody had yet asked me for my fare. Then the man said, "Cumberland Street next stop, Pat." As I made to get off, the conductress, a young woman, was near the back collecting fares. She charged me one penny. I suspected she had an Irish accent, and I was right. I saw the same one afterwards at the dancing in Clydeferry Street.

209 Florence Street was no different from thousands of other Glasgow tenements. The communal entrance called the close, the communal outside stairway, the doors with the nameplates on them on each landing—these were features common to all of them. Add to these the plethora of smells and odours—of fish and chips and other things less pleasant and you will begin to get the picture.

I was looking for the name Gallagher, and as it was not on either of the doors at ground level, nor on the first landing, I continued on up the stairs. Near the second landing I met a tall man coming down. I had been led to believe that in Glasgow you could meet with all kinds of thieves and robbers and other undesirables on those dimly lit tenement stairs, but from what I could see of him in the semi-darkness, he looked to be alright, so I spoke to him. "Excuse me sir", I stammered, "Can you tell me if a Mr Michael Gallagher lives here?", or something like that.

The man said not a word, but turning around he beckoned me to follow him. He walked up the few steps to the landing, took a key from his pocket, and opening the door with "M. Gallagher" on it he again signed for me to follow him in. I had spoken to the man I was looking for and did not know him. He had not spoken a word to me but he knew who I was. When later I asked him how he knew it was me, he said he knew me out of my mother. His daughter, Kathleen, my cousin, came in a few minutes after that. The last time I had seen her was as a small girl in Ireland with her mother some years before. Now she was a grown woman. The rest of the family were away on holiday and were due back that afternoon. Michael was actually on his way to the station to meet them when I met him on the stairs. Then he hurried away again and Kathleen made tea for me.

I was at Queen Street goods station at six-thirty in the morning as Gruddy had told me to be, presenting myself and the letter I carried to foreman Andy Wishart, a swollen little man with a tomato-red nose, and I do not think it was the severity of the Scottish climate that was the underlying cause of it. "It did not take you the whole day yesterday to come up from Stranraer, did it?" he enquired. "You should have reported here for work in the afternoon, you know." I had not known that. A bad start, said I to myself.

Andy spent nearly all of his working day, every day, marking down figures in a book he carried about with him as he went around checking on the wagons that were to be emptied and the lorries that were to be loaded with potatoes for delivering to wholesalers and shops and stores, and giving orders about where they were to go.

"Johnny Wilson will show you what to do", he told me when he had finished giving directions to the lorry driver. Johnny Wilson was even more of a nark than Andy himself. Another red-faced, bulbous-nosed, ignorant-spoken moron of a man; he was always giving orders and urging on the work without doing much of it himself—that was the kind of a man he was. At least Andy was a foreman in the yard, but Johnny was only a worker, and not a very good one at that. But he was a mate of Andy's and that stood good for him. Sometimes he went away at the midday break and came back smelling of drink, and then for a while he would be a bit more sociable (drink does not affect everybody in the same way), but as the day wore on he reverted to form. He was always very bad tempered on Saturday mornings. "Take no notice of that old buggar", said Willie Thomson, a big friendly man. "There is an old bastard like him on every job." And so there was, as I was to find out over the years, and a despicable breed they were.

I had to look for lodgings. Staying with the Gallaghers could not go on indefinitely. With four daughters and a son of her own, my aunt had no house room to spare in her two-roomed apartment. Not many people with families had enough house room for themselves never mind having any to spare in the Glasgow circles I moved into in the late nineteen-forties. And anyhow I did not want to impose upon my relations.

Martin Lavelle lived in one of the other flats on the stairs. Martin was a near neighbour from home—a Shanahee man—and though I had seen him home on holidays a few times, I had never spoken to him. He was nearer to my mother's age group than to mine and he had been away for a long time. When he heard I was in Gallagher's he came in to see me and when the subject of lodging came up he suggested I try Mochan's in Abbotsford Place. I asked him what sort of place it was. He said, "It's all right as long as you don't mind staying where there is a crowd."

"How many about would that be?" I asked.

"About twenty", he said, "and more at the weekends when the men from the hydro schemes come down."

Twenty men or more in the lodgings seemed a few too many for my liking. Sure that would be nearly as crowded as the bothy, I thought. I kept clear of Mochan's, and probably just as well; I heard a lot about the place afterwards, and not all of it complimentary by any means.

Mrs Gallagher said I should watch the shop windows for adverts; people who kept lodgers often advertised in newsagents' windows when they had vacancies. And sure enough, the next evening on my way back from work I saw the following, handwritten on a piece of paper, displayed in a newsagent's window at Gorbals Cross: FULL BOARD AND LODGINGS FOR WORKING MAN. APPLY: MRS HANNIGAN, HOSPITAL STREET. I remember thinking as I walked along to Hospital Street that maybe I would get a room to myself and wouldn't that be nice. I was innocent. I soon found out that lodgers did not have rooms to themselves in that part of the world.

I got the room alright, but I had to share it with five others, three beds in the room and two men in each bed. In the next room it was the same arrangement, and you never knew what kind of a man was going to be put in beside you. The landlady's word was law. If a man was good enough to stay the night in her house he was good enough for you to sleep with. And anyone who did not like that knew where the door was. It was either accept it or go. Nobody was forced to stay against their will.

The house had no bathroom. A small toilet served the needs of everybody, and it did not have a wash-hand basin. The kitchen sink, the "jaw box" as it was called, was used for washing and shaving as well as its for ordinary purposes. Men queued up in the hall to use the toilet and queued in the kitchen to wash and shave, and for their meals. Mrs Hannigan, an elderly woman, and an extremely busy and hard-working one, did not think men really needed hot water to shave, cold water done just as good, she said. A red-haired Mayo man who liked to be in her good books, said he had never used hot water for shaving, always cold water from the tap. Where he got water from a tap in his townland or district he did not say and I do not know, because they had no running water there at the time, except the water that ran in the seough of the road. More likely it was bog water he used, as didn't we all. She told him that was why he was so good looking, that shaving with cold water worked wonders for the complexion. The truth of the matter, as far as she was concerned, was that she did not want to have us coming in her way, boiling water. She had more than enough to do without being bothered by men looking for hot water for shaving. I only shaved twice weekly then, and soon I found it more practical to get a shave in the barber's at the corner for eightpence.

We were given sandwiches to take with us to our work for lunchtime, wrapped up in old newspaper—four slices of bread to each man, and always with something on them—cheese or tomatoes or meat of some kind. We got tea and sugar too, mixed, and packaged in smaller papers. Lodgers were discouraged from hanging about the house in the evening. Once the evening meal was over we were expected to go out and not appear again in the house until bedtime. And that was mostly what we done. I used to go to the pictures a lot, an average of four evenings a week or more. I was lucky in that I liked films, it kept me out of the pubs and was ever so much cheaper. Tenpence would get you into the better class picture house and in some it was as low as fivepence. That was for the stalls, the balcony was slightly dearer, but very seldom did I go to the balcony.

Everybody in the digs was obliged to go to Mass on Sundays, like it or not. To satisfy the landlady you had to be a chapel goer. Some pretended they were going to Mass but went up to the Barrows or to Paddy's Market instead. One man who tried passing the excuse that he had no good shirt for going to Mass only got away with it once. He was warned to have a shirt for the next Sunday or else he would not be there. "If you don't get a shirt you will get a shift." Those were her words; "I might as well have a lump of a bullock lying in there in the room as a man who won't go to Mass."

Mrs Hannigan worked very hard. She was a woman of about seventy years of age when I knew her and not only did she cook for us and look after the rooms, she washed all our clothes as well. Those were the days before people had washing machines in their houses, and when the women took the washing to the "steamie"—the public wash house. She overdid herself with work and it proved too much for her. Her husband took ill and died and between nursing him and all it got her down with the result she had to take things easy, and that meant the end of keeping lodgers for her. This happened less than two years after the time of which I now write. I hope I will be able to work until I am as old as she was, but I am afraid I will not. She was a good woman in many ways and a strong, hardy woman too, I believe, in her day. Age catches up on us all.

On my first Sunday in Glasgow Martin Lavelle took me up to "The Barras", the famous weekend open air market off the Gallowgate. I must confess the place did not impress me to any great extent. The street traders were selling their wares, shouting and bawling, endeavouring on their best to attract the public and to drown out each other's voices. I did not think there was anything wonderful about the whole thing, but I did not say that to Martin as I did not want to offend him. He was a decent man and it was nice of him to show me around. I asked him how long he had been in Glasgow. "Twenty years", he said, "and never spent a day idle." Twenty years! Surely I thought that was a long time and a great record. Little did I think then that over forthy years later I would still be in Glasgow, and still be working, as bad as the first day.

It was not very long before I found out that the overwhelming majority of Irish people in Glasgow were from the County Donegal. A few could be found from other northern counties and there were quite a number from the Belmullet district of Mayo, more so than from any other part of the West, nearly all of them ex-tattie hokers who had come to settle in the city, though they might not all be keen to admit it—tattie hokers not being a breed who were looked up to. You could on occasion meet the odd stray man or woman from almost any county in Ireland, but Donegal swamped out all of them together. Scottish people who did not know the geographical outlay of Ireland

96

could be forgiven for thinking that Donegal was bigger than the rest of the country put together, and some of them actually did think that.

No wonder the Donegal men monopolised all the navvying jobs; they had to, from sheer force of numbers. So strong were they numerically that socially they had themselves organised into district groupings, such as the Rosses Association, the Gweedore Club, and others. They had their favourite streets to live in, and their favourite pubs to drink in, and their favourite chapels to worship in, such as, St John's in the Gorbals. I got on comparatively well with them from the start, but maybe that was because I was not much of a threat to them workwise, or any other wise for that matter. Men from other counties did not like them and were not loath to say so. "Oh, them young lads in Hannigan's are alright, they are not trained into it yet", one man said, "wait until you meet the real thick ignorant Donegal man, then you will know."

One thing I found hard to stand with the Donegal people, both men and women, was how they talked as if they thought Mayo was just a townland or a village when they should have known it was a big county, one of the biggest in Ireland. They would enquire with me after the welfare of so and so from Mayo, some person they had known or worked with somewhere. How was he or she getting on? Were they at home now? Did they get married?—that kind of talk. When I would say I did not know who they were talking about, they expressed surprise. "You should know them, they were from Mayo." And them talking about someone who belonged to a place maybe seventy or eighty miles away from where I was from.

Another thing I discovered before long was that I could recognise other Irishmen from the look of them. No matter how long they had been away from Ireland you could still recognise them from their appearance and from the way they walked. When I mentioned this to a man in the digs, himself an Irishman, he said, "You can take the man out of the bog, but you can never take the bog out of the man." I don't think that was the right explanation. It was, I would say, a lot more the look of the countryman they had about them that made them look different in the city. A Dublin man would not stick out near as much in the streets of Glasgow as a Donegal or a Mayo man would. And as regards the way they walked, I think people whose formative years were spent in stepping over the springy flexible sward will always have about them as they go along, a different gait to those who learned to walk on hard recalcitrant city pavements.

The other blokes in the digs were all employed on public works—building and civil engineering projects. Not only were they earning considerably more money than I was, they did not start work until eight o'clock in the morning, whereas I had to be on the job at six-thirty. They were still asleep in bed when I was already working and they were finished as early in the evenings as I was. If only I could get on the public works the same as them I would be alright—I would be "on the pig's back", or so I thought. But there was not a hope of that and all because I had come into the country on an "agricultural passport". Passports were required for travel between Great Britain and Éire in those days, and I, having come over to engage in farm work, had "agricultural worker" marked on mine and my employment cards were for "agricultural work only". So like it or not I had to stick to work of an agricultural nature for a least one year, after which time I stood a chance of getting the cards changed. That was the rule though some managed to get around it, but not always in a legal manner.

One night, after I had been in Hannigan's for a week of two, one of the men who slept in the other room came into ours. I was already in bed as I had to rise very early in the morning; the others had not yet come in. He sat on the chair beside the bed and began to talk. "I hear you are hobbled with them ould agricultural cards", he said. He was a Cavan man and the Cavan people refer to almost everything as "ould", be it old or new. "I know where you can get a right set of ould cards", he went on. It would be in a public house called the Boreen Bar in Bedford Street, he told me. If I were to go down there any night and ask for a barman named Tony; that was the man who could get them for me. But I was to speak to the guy quietly, make sure nobody heard me asking him. Tony was alright; he would get them for me he assured me. Five pounds they would cost and it would be well worth it because once I had the cards I could start work anywhere. "You can go into any kind of work then", my Cavan friend informed me. But there was a snag to it. It might not be my own name that would be on the cards, he said.

"Whose name would be on them?" I asked.

"The name of whoever the cards belonged to first", he told me. "You will have to work under his name. That is if the cards were used before. Sometimes he has new sets, but they would be dearer."

I believe the man meant all right. He probably thought he was doing me a favour, but I was not attracted to the idea, and certainly not if it was going to mean working on another man's cards and under another man's name. How Tony came to have national insurance cards to sell I did not ask and I was not told. I thought it better to soldier on the way I was and so I never went to the Boreen Bar. Afterwards I was to find out that the practice of working on somebody else's cards was fairly widespread among Irishmen and women in Scotland. One man I knew was working night shift using the cards of a man who had gone back to Ireland, while drawing benefit from his own in the labour exchange. He was not the only one. Another, in a similar situation got found out and sent to jail for it, and him being Irish the papers gave it a big write-up. "Paddy's two card trick", they called his game.

Down the country our wages were paid to us in loose cash, a bad way if ever there was one. That was not the ganger's fault; it was sent out to him like that from the office—a bag of cash which he dispensed to the workers like a man dealing out playing cards. A more unsatisfactory method of paying workers would be hard to find, and it gave rise to numerous rumours, complaints, and suspicions. Some maintained that for every pound the ganger gave the workers, he kept another pound for himself. I don't think it was ever that bad, but I do know the system was open to no end of temptation. The gangers were not saints but as far as I know the majority of them did not make that much out of it. In my experience the ganger was only small fry compared to the merchant. He was the real shark, the man who made the money from underpaid, underaged and overworked Irish labourers. The Scottish potato merchant was a hard-hearted, and tight-fisted man, and the closer one got to him the more one came to know him and the less one came to respect him.

In the station we began work at half-past six in the morning, except on Saturdays when we started at six. Saturday morning was the busiest time of the week as they wanted everything off to an extra early start. Finishing time was five in the evenings during the week and twelve noon on Saturdays. My pay was four pounds a week, the same as I had down the country, so the ganger had not been fiddling me, whatever else he might have done. Here we got our pay in envelopes, not in loose cash. Four pounds was supposed to be my pay, but there was no four pounds in the envelope by the time I got it. The income tax man had taken his cut out of it by then, and small as it was before, it was smaller after him. I had never heard of a code number; I did not know what a code number was or even that such a thing existed. Nobody had bothered telling me anything about income tax. Down the country I missed the ten shillings tax that was kept from me every week, but I missed it more in Glasgow and that was because I had far more outgo and expense than I had when I was working in the squad. When the income tax and the price of the insurance stamp were deducted from my four pounds I came out with three pounds and a few shillings in my pay envelope. The landlady took thirty shillings of that and I was left with a little over another thirty shillings all to myself for the whole week. I wasn't going to save much money out of that. To keep going was hard, to save anything, impossible.

It was in the middle of my third week at the station that I told the foreman I wanted a rise in wages. He seemed annoyed that I should have the temerity to bring up the subject, said he could do nothing about it, which I suppose was true for him, and told me that if that was how I felt I had better go down to the office and have a word with the merchant himself. I did just that.

The first man I met there was a youth of about sixteen, very well dressed, wearing a nice little suit and a collar and tie. He was in all probability the office boy, but in my naivety I thought that as he looked a bit on the young side to be the merchant, he was so well turned out he must be the merchant's son. He did not wait to hear my story, which I started to blabber out to him, but ushered me into a room where a few women sat at desks. I then started explaining my predicament to them, but I don't think they understood hardly a word of what I was saying. Anyhow, one of them showed me into an inner sanctum where a man sat at a large desk or table facing the door, and with a woman at a side desk typing away for all she was worth. He was a thin, sickly-looking man, the kind you would think at first sight would not say boo to a goose. But looks can be deceiving. He was able to put me in my place. I soon found out that I was wasting my time talking to him.

"It is as good for you as it is for everybody else", he said, taking off his glasses and observing me out of yellow jaundiced-looking eyes. "If you had it any better in Ireland you should have stayed there", he continued, when he had taken my measure.

That was enough to make me lose my temper. I remember saying that his whole set-up was rotten from one end of it to the other, and that the bothies down the country were not fit for humans to live in, as they were infested with rats and mice. "You are telling a lie, young man", he said, "you do not get the two together; where there are rats there are never any mice." Evidently he was an authority on the subject.

I told him I was giving in my notice, that I was leaving on Friday. "Very well, there are plenty more where you came from", was his reply. "Now get out of the office before I call the police. If they come you will go to jail", said he, putting a skinny hand on the phone beside him. So I left Mr Scrooge and his female companion to their devices. Some years later I read about his death in the papers. He had amassed a huge fortune from the labour of Irish men, women and children, although it did not say that outright in the paper. It did say, in deference to his frugality, that he had had the same overcoat for twenty years.

Back at the station I made it known to the foreman that I would be leaving on Friday. He did not let on he heard me, instead he gave directions about a lorry that was to be loaded, muttering something about making up for lost time. The following morning I was a bit late in coming in. I could not care less now. It was about seven o'clock when I walked into the station. The foreman came over, pointing up with his thumb to the big clock on the wall.

"Do you know what time it is?" he asked.

"Sorry, my watch is slow" said I, by way of answer. "It stopped during the night; I only put it going by guesswork." This of course was not true. I did not own a watch.

"We come and go by the clock up there, not by your watch", I was told. "I bet your watch won't be slow this evening." For peace sake I thought it better to say no more, just to carry on as best I could for the two days that were left.

We had no lying time on the job. When a person got his pay on Friday that was him paid up until that evening. So the fact that I was leaving did not mean I would have extra money in my pocket. Still, I had four pounds, the same as when I left home in June. The three pounds odd I had coming on Friday would make it up to over seven—enough to pay the landlady and tide me over the immediate future. But long term prospects were not promising, stuck as I was with the agricultural cards. As the fellas used to say about getting into public works, "getting the books is the trouble". By books they meant national insurance cards for building and civil engineering work. Glasgow was not the best place in the world to go looking for agriculture work and it was getting a bit late in the year for to try my luck down the country again. However, with the blessed optimism of youth I was confident that something would come up.

But things got worse before they got better. Friday evening on opening my pay envelope I found within it not the three pounds I was expecting but one ten shilling note—fifty pence in todays money—some shillings in silver, and a typewritten letter with my employer's name and the address and phone number of his office at the top. This was to inform me that as I was leaving of my own accord before the end of the season I was "in breach of contract". Therefore, they were deducting from my wages what it cost to take me over from Ireland—the sum of two pounds and ten shillings. So that was that.

On leaving the station I did not wait for the tram that would take me over to the south side. I walked down Buchanan Street and across St Enoch Square, making for the Suspension Bridge. So preoccupied was I with my thoughts that, stepping into Clyde Street at the Post Office corner, I collided bang on, amidships, with a pram overloaded with clothes and pushed by an immensely fat woman. First, she let out a torrent of the most obscene expressions, such as I had never heard a woman give voice to before, as she struggled to prevent her load from tumbling on to the pavement. Then all of a sudden her attitude changed, she got very concerned about me, asking me if I was all right, was I sure I was not hurt. With my help she straightened up her load, tied it agin with the tangled twine, and went on her way. She would have been a hawker from the rag markets around the Bridgegate (Briggate), most likely a kind woman at heart, but toughened by the life she led, like myself, a victim of circumstances over which she had little control.

That night I went along to the Paragon pictures house in Cumberland Street as I did nearly every Friday night. Frank Murray, who was my uncle, my mother's brother, was the doorman there. Frank could let a person in for nothing if he felt like it, and one time he would surely feel that way was on Friday nights after the nine o'clock interval when himself and Charlie Kelly, the other male attendant, had refreshed themselves with a couple of pints in Roper's across the road.

The Paragon did not cost much to get into anyway, eightpence in the stalls and a shilling in the balcony. It was a strange sort of picture house—an old church converted into a cinema and with the wooden pews still there being used as seats. It was a rough and rowdy place.

Frank and Charlie were two hardy and courageous men, and they needed to be, working in that place. Whenever a "rammy" started non-combatants jumped up and stood on the seats while the fighting raged all over the place. Frank and Charlie wouldn't be long coming over from Roper's then, and into the thick of it, trying to put them out of the hall. Sometimes an accomplice on the inside would open one or other of the side doors and let in a whole lot of undesirables who had been hanging around outside, and then it was pandemonium, with the attendants rushing around all through the hall, locating them and flinging them out again.

The two side doors also served as a handy escape route for the neds whenever the police came in after them. Once outside they fled like hell down side streets and alleyways with the coppers in hot pursuit. Then it was woe betide any child or old person who came in the way of either hunted or hunters, they were unceremoniously knocked down in the mad headlong chase. Often the police, frustrated at losing their quarry would grab a few uninvolved youngsters who happened to be about and throw them into the van. After spending the night, or maybe the weekend, in the cells, they came up before the Magistrate, all dishevelled, and dirty, and guilty looking, charged with breach of the peace, or police assault, or both, or something else. Then it was a fine, or if they had been in trouble before maybe a spell in jail, to emerge as embittered and avowed enemies of everything to do with law and order. And many a time all because they had been in the wrong place at the wrong time. It was rough around the Paragon.

It was Frank who told me that I might have a chance of getting work with Pinkerton, the rhubarb grower out at Hogganfield Loch. I went out there on the number seven tram from Ballater Street first thing next morning and having got off at the loch I saw the farm entrance and went in.

John Pinkerton, a man of about seventy years of age, did not look like my idea of a farmer. Of medium height and build, and pale of face, he wore a navy blue suit and had on a winged white collar and a tie. "I could give you a few days", he replied slowly, when I asked him if there was any chance of work. "I have a bit of delving needing done", he told me, "a few places the tractor is not able to get at, bits of corners and that, ye ken, you should be good with a spade."

I don't think I had ever heard the word "delving" before. It was not a word that was used around our place at home, and at first something silly in me made me connect it in my mind with diving, but when he mentioned a spade I knew then it was digging he was talking about. "I'll give you fifteen shillings a day, paid every evening", he said in his unhurried way. Come out on Monday morning at half-past seven, I was told. Finishing time would be half-five in the evening.

I had found work. It might only be for a few days but it was something. I was happy and well pleased. I made up my mind I would work well for Pinkerton, and with a bit of luck he might keep me longer than a few days. I was there in good time on Monday morning.

CHAPTER THIRTEEN

Rhubarb and Mushrooms

PINKERTON'S HAD ABOUT three hundred acres under rhubarb, and in addition to that they were the biggest mushroom growers in Scotland. In the busy season they employed about sixty workers or more, mostly women, out in the fields and in the mushroom sheds. The gaffer over the rhubarb gathering was Jock Welch. To me he looked an old man, though I do not think he could have been much over fifty at the time, but a man of fifty looks old in a young person's eyes. The rhubarb women always referred to him as "Big Jock". He was not a tall man, no more than average height, but he was broad, and with a thick neck which made his head look small, and strong round shoulders and thick arms. In a vague way he reminded me of pictures of male lions and buffaloes that I had seen—all strength and brawn in the foreparts. Jock was nearly always chewing tobacco and spitting, and he had a most scurrilous tongue; every sentence he uttered was spiced with swear words. He was an Orangeman, and a bitter one, with a twisted mind with regards Catholics and especially Catholic priests. He could say some very provoking things, and sometimes he was egged on to it—baited, to get him going. He was not a bad man to work under, because at the back of his hateful way he was not a sharp man. I knew men with less to say who were a lot worse.

Jock's son, Willie, or "Wully" as his father pronounced his name, worked there driving one of the lorries, and there was also his son-in-law Charlie, a carter. Jock never tired of praising those two, bumming them up to the ninety-nines, boasting about the good men and great workers they were. I never saw anything extraordinary about either of them, nor did I ever hear them say much in his favour.

About forty women worked in Pinkerton's fields, most of them from the Blackhill estate, adjoining the farm. Five and a half days a week, from seven-thirty to five-thirty, and twelve on Saturday, they toiled, pulling rhubarb, weighing it into one stone bundles, loading it on to the carts to take it into the farmyard, and there re-loading it on to lorries to be taken away to the railway station. And a tough lot those women were, well able to exchange obscenities with any man, even with Jock Welch.

My job most of the time was digging, or "delving" as old John called it. After a few weeks he asked me for my employment cards and that was a sign that I would be there for some time; yet he still continued to pay me every evening. I was not the only one to be paid in that way. Several others as well as myself lined up at the window every evening to be handed out their day's wages. It was not a way that was conducive to saving money, but I was always careful with money and not only did I manage to keep going on what I was getting, I managed to put a little away every week. He never kept income tax off me and that was a good help.

Alec Faulds drove the big Massey-Ferguson tractor. Alec was a nice man, gentle, and easy to get along with, and very good with his hands. He was able to fix the tractor and the lorries when anything went wrong with them; he could turn his hand to almost anything, a real handyman.

The two horses and carts of the farm worked full-time, every day, at one thing or another, usually drawing in rhubarb. The smaller of the horses, "Belgie", was worked by Eddie MacGill, a lad of about eighteen, a big red cheeked youth whom I remembered as having been always in a good mood. You could hear him any length away, singing and whistling as he worked, and bantering with the women, much to the annoyance of Jock Welch. The other carter, who worked "Bob", the big horse, was Jock's son-in-law, Charlie MacNaught. He was not altogether as foul-mouthed as Jock, but he thought along the same lines. He was a bully who would make it hard for someone he thought was afraid of him or was not able to stand up to him. A punch-up took place one day between him and a man named John Bain due to a difference of opinion regarding which of then was the rightful owner of a pair of oilskin trousers. He made to hit Bain but got hit himself instead. Charlie went down and when he got up he made another rush at Bain and got punched hard and good a second time and then he went down even quicker than the first time. He had picked on the wrong man and after that he never laid hands on anything belonging to John Bain again. He did complain to Pinkerton's son, Matthew, hoping to get Bain the sack (strictly speaking the oilskins were Pinkerton's property). But Matthew said it had nothing to do with him and they should settle it between themselves. They had already done that. Charlie had a dressing of sticking plaster on his nose for a week and that was the end of the matter.

Jock and Charlie lived in the two tied cottages inside the main entrance to the farm. Could be they were too close for comfort, those two irascible men, for they were never done in—fighting and bickering among themselves, always "chewing the fat" about something.

Another old man who thought of himself as a bit of a gaffer there was Bill Bryson. Bill must have been a man close to seventy as he had been in the Boer War fifty years before, but he was still a strong able-bodied man and well able to do a day's work. He was not liked by the workers as he had the name of being an informer—carrying tales to the boss. The few times I worked with him we hit it off all right; I could not say a word against the man, though I do not know what he might have said about me. A strong dislike existed between him and Jock Welch, caused, it was said, by a contention which took place some time previous as to who would get the house Charlie was in. The house had been vacant and Bill wanted it for his son. Jock wanted it for Charlie. Charlie got the house and came to live in it and to work for Pinkerton, and that, according to the gossip, accounted for the ill-feeling.

We had an hour for our tea break every day at noon. Having filled our cans at the urn in one of the sheds we sat down to eat our snack anywhere convenient. For a time some of us sat on bales of straw in another shed. That was fine until a flea-invested load of straw came in and then we were not long getting out of there. Boy Oh! Could them fleas not jump. Paddy Caulfield said that if people could jump like fleas we would have no need for public transport.

Paddy was a Belmullet man the same as myself but much older, very much older. He was over a long time. Fifty years it was, he said, since he came to Scotland, and he had never once been back. The idea of taking a trip home had never occurred to him. I found it hard to understand that it was the people and the things connected with years and years before that he was interested in more than the present, especially where Ireland was concerned. I know better now when I am getting like that myself.

Paddy's regular workmate, Sam Galloway, was another man out of his generation in that he had put through his hands a number of wives, or women who acted the part of wives; one, it was said, for

107

every few years. Nowadays they would be called "common-law wives". Paddy Caulfield called them "old hairpins". Jock Welch had other names for them. Sam was a harmless poor old soul; I think the women had been using him as a meal ticket, and in return for their keep they warmed his bed. Paddy and Sam were both retired men who supplemented their pensions with the money they got from John Pinkerton for hoeing and weeding and forking all day between long rows of rhubarb plants. They were only two of several old age pensioners working there.

The mushroom growing side of the business was operated by Pinkerton junior—the son, Matthew, a man in his mid thirties. It would be hard to find anywhere more of a contrast between the ways and manners of two men as there was between those two, father and son. While the old man was cool and unhurried in his ways, Matthew was a rumbustious hurricane, always blustering and rushing about, never giving people time to finish what they were doing properly, and seldom satisfied.

One day he came to where I was working and took me away to help load boxes of mushrooms on to a lorry. After I was loading for a few minutes he yelled that I was not moving fast enough, pulled the box out of my hands and flung it on to the lorry with such force the box burst open and the mushrooms scattered everywhere. I loaded no more. I walked back to my work and left him and his women to it. I was working for the old man and buggar Matthew and his mad hashing. He never kept up the hashing himself for very long; he soon got tired of it and went off to something else. But he expected others to keep it up the whole time.

The main ingredient used for the growing of mushrooms was horse's dung, well rotted, and preferably with plenty of straw through it. One of the two lorries of the farm did little else but to collect horse manure from stables all around Glasgow and in the surrounding countryside. Horses were common then, not like now, and their manure was plentiful and easy to get. I remember one day a load came in with a whole lot of timber shavings and sawdust mixed through it and Matthew, when he saw it, was so angry, he nearly threw a fit. I never saw any man who could get worked up into such a state when something annoyed him. The old man impishly asked if it had come from the wooden horse of Troy, but Matt was not amused. No more manure came from the south-side sawmills stables.

Pinkerton's in their heyday had fifty sheds producing mushrooms a shed for every week of the year. Today there are no mushrooms on Hogganfield Farm, nor any rhubarb. There is no Hogganfield Farm any more. As Mrs Matt Pinkerton said to me when I called to see the old place in 1984: "It is all gone now." Barratt's have built houses all over where it once stood.

One Saturday evening two young Donegal lads came to Hannigan's to stay the weekend. They were O'Donnell and Campbell, both aged about sixteen, but they did not look their ages; they were small for their years. They had been working out the country with some tattie hoking squad and were now *en route* home, it being the season's end. Having decided to spend the weekend in Glasgow to sample the pleasures of the city, someone directed them to Hannigan's. Next day they went to the Barrows and round about sightseeing, and that night they came along with me to the Irish dancing in Stobcross Street. So well did they enjoy the city and what it had to offer they fell at once under its spell. "Brave crack in Glasgow", was their agreed comment. Now they announced that instead of going on the Derry boat Monday night as planned, they would like to stay on, if only they could get work. I took them out with me to Pinkerton's to see if there was anything doing, and the old man put them to work right away. They turned out to be two gallant little workers. That was the time of year (late November) for taking in rhubarb to be grown in forced conditions in the heated sheds during the winter and they took to it like ducks to the water—digging it up, loading it on to carts—they tore in with a heart and a half. And, like MacGill, they sang and whistled at their work. In those days that was a regular thing; people must have been happier at their work then.

Coming near Christmas my mother wrote asking me home, and that put the notion into my head. Before I got the letter I had no intention of going but I changed my mind and I could not get away soon enough—I was counting the days. It was from Jimmy Price, a Swinford man who stayed in the digs with us, that I bought the ticket. With Jimmy it was the other way round; he had got the ticket to go, and now he wasn't going, so I bought it from him, and that suited both of us.

I walked down to the Broomielaw carrying a heavy canvas bag with a zip fastner that I had bought at Paddy's Market. My old suitcase had given up the ghost. As we sailed down the Clyde I overheard one man, a seasonal harvest worker, say to another man beside him that it was as fine an evening for that time of year as ever he had been on the boat, and I wondered to myself how many times he had made the crossing. It was known for harvest workers from Ireland to have crossed the Irish Sea a hundred times, and more— twice yearly for their whole working lives.

Sixteen hours it took us until we pulled in at the North Wall in Dublin. The boat was not crowded and I stretched myself out across two seats and with my bag under my head for a pillow and my coat over me I was quite comfortable and slept most of the night. On the quay the jarvies with their horse-drawn cabs were waiting, each wanting us to go with himself. You would almost think from the way they carried on that they were the husbands of the women who had pounced on us when we came off the bus by the Liffeyside in June. So I had no problem in getting transport to take me to Westland Row, and there I boarded the train for the west.

Night had fallen by the time I reached Ballina and it was damp and cold and the buildings looked smaller than I had remembered them to be. When I had passed that way before I thought Ballina was a big place, now it didn't look much of a place at all.

The first man I met when I came off the bus in Belmullet was my neighbour from Morahan, Jamsey MacNamara. He had come into the town in the hope that Sonny, his brother, might be on the bus. He was not. Sonny had been one of our number when we went away on that memorable morning, and I had not seen him nor heard tidings of him since we parted two days later at Glasgow's Broomielaw, when he went away to Fife with Francie Cooney. Sonny and Jamsey are dead now. Both passed away in late middle age. They were fine young men, and nice fellows wherever you met them; they were the kind of men who would stick up for a friend in trouble or help one in need. We went into John Doherty's and there we had a couple of drinks and then we came down home to Morahan in Doherty's car, with MacNamara's bicycle tied on the back.

Mary Jo was asleep when I came in. She had gone to bed on the condition that she would be woken up when I showed up. She had missed me a lot while I was away and was always asking when would I come home. They told me that for weeks after I went she used to go up to the high ground behind the house and call out my name as loud as she could, hoping that I might hear her and come home. And first thing in the morning she would go up to the room and look in my bed to see if I had come during the night. We did not have Teresa and Eileen at that time; they did not arrive on the scene until the late fifties. My mother fostered out Teresa to be a younger sister for Mary Jo, and when she saw Eileen with her blond hair she fell for her and fostered her as well.

Mary Jo was delighted that I was home. She said her prayers had been answered and God had sent me home for Christmas. It was hard to get her to go back to sleep again that night, and she was up in the morning before any of us to go and tell Paddy Pack the good news. Mary Jo has come a long way since then.

My Local Defence Force uniform was still there in the room, hanging on the wall at the foot of the bed, as my mother said, waiting for me to come home. She had covered it over with an old raincoat to keep the dust off. That house is empty now; cold, deserted and lonely, with no father or mother to welcome me home. Mary Jo and Paddy Pack and I have long since gone our separate ways. But the nail is still there in the wall where my mother hung that green uniform to await my return from Scotland. It is only a small thing but it saddened me very much the last time I saw it.

I had plenty new finery home with me, so much of it that my bag was bulging. In addition to the grey suit I had when I went, and which I had recently got cleaned and was now looking better than ever I had seen it, I had another rig-out—a black and white check sports jacket and grey flannel trousers bought at the autumn sales in Burtons of Argyle Street, the tailors of taste, as they styled themselves in their advertisements. I had also a gaberdine coat that wasn't new; it was a second-hand buy from the Barrows. And I had a fine pair of red shoes, a green pullover and a garish scarf of many colours. And that scarf was worn more for show-off than anything else. I had working gear as well, an ex-army khaki jerkin and trousers from the army and navy stores, and a black velvet beret. Black berets were very popular in those days. That was before they became associated in the public eye with paramilitary organisations. At that time they were more iden-tified with Montgomery's Eight Army. I recall one fellow who worked with us with Wimpey about 1950, a west Galway lad by the name of McDonagh, and because he always wore a black beret over a longish nose we gave him the nickname "Monty", short for Montgomery, and he took no offence at the name, in fact he answered to it.

My mother said I would not have as much if I had stayed in

Morahan and my father said I had enough to do me until I got married. He was well pleased with the black leather leggings I had for him, the very thing he needed, he said, for wearing around the haggard and the stables, to keep the muck off the bottoms of his trousers.

I cycled into town the day after I came home. Every person I met stopped to speak to me and I came off the bike and we shook hands. And each of them said nearly the same thing but with slight variations. It was either: "You're welcome home", or, "when did you come home", or, "was it last night you came"—almost as if it had been rehearsed. The same hand-shaking and welcoming-home ritual took place again outside the chapel before and after Mass on Christmas Day. It wasn't as if I was any kind of a celebrity any more than anybody else. Everybody who came home was welcomed and greeted by the people.

I stayed at home longer that year than I had intended to stay. I thought it would only be for a fortnight but I was there until the middle of March, almost three months. My mother said: "stay where you are now until the days lengthen." And I did that. January and February can be two bad months for anyone working out under the mercy of the elements, and everybody engaged in outside work knows that well. So I stayed at home until the days lengthened.

A general election took place in Ireland in February of that year (on the fourth I think it was held), and during the run up to it I became involved in a small way with the new political party, Clann na Poblachta. The Clann, as we called ourselves, was challenging the old pair, Fianna Fáil and Fine Gael, who saw the new party as so much of a threat to their game of monopoly, that for a while they almost forgot their quarrels in order to concentrate against the new menace. "Communists and red upstarts" they called the new crowd.

Three candidates were fielded by Clann na Poblachta in North Mayo in that election. They were Dr Michael Hardy of Foxford, Martin MacGrath of Ballina, and Michael Joe Hefferon of Aughleam. Dr Hardy went within an ace of being elected; MacGrath and Hefferon polled well too. In all, the Clann got ten members elected into the Dáil, but only one west of the Shannon. I joined the new party because I was attracted to its progressive and forward-looking ideas, and also to the charisma of some of its leading figures, like its founder Seán MacBride, and young Dr Noel Browne.

I recall that February well. It was wild blustery weather with fierce westerly gales blowing in from the Atlantic, gales fit nearly to blow

112

myself and the old bike off the road, as I went around at night in the wind and the rain, sticking up election posters with wet flour on walls and telegraph poles all over the parish. It was not a usual thing around Erris for someone as young as I was to come out as a political activist, though I have seen plenty of the young ones at it here in Glasgow, and why shouldn't they? The future is theirs. I started young in that way.

I was mainly instrumental in organising a branch of Clann na Poblachta in our area, myself and Pat Lally of Aughalasheen. Pat became chairman of the branch, with myself as secretary, and Patrick Dixon as a lukewarm treasurer. After I went away again my father took over as secretary, but I don't think the branch was affiliated for a second year. Clann na Poblachta did not enjoy a long life and our part in it was small.

I well remember the Sunday nights of that year when we used to cycle miles to dance halls. We would go from Morahan in crowds, boys and girls mixed, back to Walsh's in Drum, and down to Derrynameel to Davie Lally's; we even went out to Bangor a few times; every Sunday night we went somewhere. Of course, that was not the only year it was done; it had been going on for a number of years, but it was the last year I ever did it. I also recall having no lights on our bikes which was against the law. The Guards would wait along the road, in order to catch us on our way home in the small hours of the morning. I was twice lucky not to have been charged. The first time I was let off with a warning, and the second time I cycled right through the checkpoint and escaped, and though Carty, an affable Guard, called after me in name, telling me that I would not get away with it, I never heard any more about it. Some of my fellow travellers that night were not so lucky, they were summoned before the District Court and fined five shillings each for riding unlighted bicycles at night.

Ash Wednesday always put an end to the nocturnal dancing-related activities for a while. Dancing during Lent was forbidden by the Church and so the halls remained closed, except on St Patick's night; a dispensation was allowed for that night, and after that they were banned again until Easter Sunday. But I was not around for Easter. I was back in Glasgow by then.

I cycled the six miles into Belmullet for the bus the morning I left, with my bag behind me on the carrier, and I left the bike in Hurst's yard to be collected by Brian Carey when he went in later in the day to sign for his dole. I took the train from Ballina to Dublin, and then out to Dun Laoghaire, crossed on the Holyhead boat, got a train to Crewe, and changed there for Glasgow. This roundabout odyssey was undertaken to avoid spending a night in Dublin, but what I gained in one way I lost in another. It was a long tiresome run and it was late afternoon the following day when we pulled into Glasgow Central. I never travelled that way again.

Getting lodgings again in Mrs Hannigan's house was easy. As she said herself she would not see any right man stuck for want of a place to lie down. If she did not have a room she would make room and no bed in her house was left without its two occupants. No sooner was one man gone than another came. Many a time I came in from work in the evening to find a strange suitcase lying in the room and then I would be wondering what like of a man belonged to that case, and more so if I knew he was going to be put into bed with me. It was the same in every digs, and some were a lot worse than Hannigan's. In Mochan's in Abbotsford Place, it was said, the beds were on double shift—the night workers sleeping in them during the day, and the day shift men in them at night.

This time I was put into the recess bed beside Jim Canning from Leitrim. I liked that bed; it was comfortable, as were all her beds when they were not overcrowded, but whenever three were put in the same bed, that was a bit too much for comfort. I never liked having to take pot luck as regards bed-mates in lodgings. And yet I do not think I fared too badly in that way. The worst I had to endure was from a bloke who kept grinding his teeth in his sleep all night, and he did not remember anything about it once he woke up, or so he claimed. People who snore in their sleep don't know they do it either, and it's another annoying thing, and believe me I had to put up with a few snorers in my time. But it could have been worse. If heed could be paid to what some men said one could come across queer hawks of bed-mates, trying unmentionable acts in bed during the night, and knowing the world as I now do, I do not doubt, but that a lot of what was said could be true.

I got back working with Pinkerton's as well. Even in the few months I was away there had been changes. The two young Donegal lads had departed, both from there and from Hannigan's; where to, nobody seemed to know for sure. In Pinkerton's it was said they had gone back to Ireland, and in Hannigan's it was said they had gone north to work on Pitchlochary dam. Anyhow, they were not around any more, and I never saw or heard of them again, whatever became of them.

John Pinkerton's age was coming against him; he was not involving himself with as much of the work as he had been, and that caused a few of us to be put on to different tasks. Matthew, thinking more along modernisation lines than his old man, bought a small mechanical cultivator. This was used not only for scuffing between the rows of plants where Caulfield and Galloway and others spent many a day, it also took over the digging of the small areas left after the tractor. I maintain to this day that that machine did not do the work half as thoroughly as we had been doing it by hand, but such is progress.

Sam operated the cultivator and it became his pride and joy. Paddy said that the cultivator was Sam's wee monkey. He certainly loved playing with it; he got as much from working it, I think, as any little boy would have got from playing with a toy monkey. The machine took years off Sam; instead of getting older, he started getting younger looking since he was put working it.

Matthew decided that the sheds, all fifty plus of them, needed a new coat of tar on the outsides. The first man commissioned to carry out this work was a youth named John Delargy, but he did not last long at it. He and Matthew had a blazing row. I think it was because he was caught sitting down when he should have been working, and he either left or got fired, or a mixture of both. He said himself he was packing it in; Matt said he was sacking him, and although they were both shouting loud I don't know which of them declared his intention first. But at the end of the row Delargy left and then I was put on to the job. Matt offered it to me on a piece work basis—"So you won't fucking dodge, same as that cunt did."

Some of those sheds were huge old structures of about fifty or more yards long and half as wide. Three pounds he gave me for every big shed I tarred, and two pounds for the smaller ones—the ex-army huts. It was good weather, very suitable for the job. I earned an average of nine pounds for each week that I was at it, and that was good money in 1948.

With all his impatience and his bustle Matt was not bad to work under once one got to know him. Like most people he had his good points. It was the cheeky aggressive way he had about him was the worst part of him. And he would address me as "Paddy" when he knew well that was not my name. This I did not like. To my way of thinking people are entitled to be called their right names. This addressing of every Irishman as "Paddy" is, and always was, I believe, far more prevalent in England than in Scotland.

The tarring of the sheds did not agree with me healthwise. Before many weeks had passed I had a crop of boils on my neck and arms, something I never had before, and they were most painful and annoying. Mrs Hannigan's son, Frank, drew out the first one (on the back of the neck it was) by pressing a heated bottle open neck down over it, and the suckage of the heated glass drew the corrupt matter out of the boil and into the bottle. It was an unorthodox and torturous operation that he had learned to perform when he was a sailor, and it did not help, for though that boil disappeared several others came and they all but crippled me. With the pain and discomfort I spent some sleepless nights, but still I struggled on with my work. I tried different remedies, until at last, when everything else had failed, I went to the doctor. He gave me ointment and bandages, a sling to put my arm in, and a bottle to take as tonic. Also, he put me on the sick list, and more than that, he ordered me to quit working with tar.

It was hard on me then. To pay the landlady I had to dip into the few pounds savings I had. All I got off the sick benefit was only a pittance and would not half pay my digs. Some people would say those were the good old days, but they were not; they were the bad old days. They were the tail-end of the times when people who did not have the money to pay for their medical treatment went without it. The finest thing that ever happened in Britain came into being later in that year of 1948, namely Aneurin Bevan's Health Service Bill.

CHAPTER FOURTEEN

"Building and Civil Engineering"

IT WAS EDDIE O'BRIEN, a Donegal lad, who told me about the housing estate that John Lawrence was building at Carntyne. He said they were looking for men to dig founds. So I went to Springboig, that was the name of the site, and saw the man in charge of the labour force. His name was Alex Carson, a small middle-aged man wearing ex-army gear like a lot of working men did at that time, an ordinary-looking bloke for a foreman. I asked him for a job and mentioned that it was agricultural cards I had. He made no comment one way or the other, but pulling out a notebook from his pocket he asked me my name and how to spell it. Then, with a short stub of pencil, which he wet in his mouth to make it write better, he laboriously wrote: "For John Lawrence, Builders, Springboig Scheme. We wish to put Bearer John Carey to work as a general labourer. Please oblige with cards." And he signed it, "A. Carson, Foreman Ganger". Then he tore out the page and gave it to me, telling me that I was to take it to my labour exchange, together with my insurance cards and they would fix me up with "the right cards", and that I was to report for work at the office up the road at eight o'clock next morning.

Next I called at Pinkerton's to collect my cards. I had to hang around for a while, waiting, as Matthew had gone out somewhere in the car. I was talking to John Bain when suddenly he arrived back, in a hurry as usual. "Have you not got anything better to do than coming in here wasting the men's time?" he asked as he breezed out of the car. "When are you going to start work?" I told him that I was starting work on the morrow, with Lawrence the builder, and that I had come for my cards. "You won't get as much money from the builder as you have been getting from me", was his remark as we walked towards the house. He went into the house and shortly reappeared with the cards. Another man was on one of the sheds, tarring—a new man. A Pole, Bain told me he was, a small stumpy man. He could have his tarring.

The man in the labour exchange was civil, far more so than his counterparts in Ireland who thought they were big shots because they sat writing with a pencil and another pencil stuck behind their ears. He took my old cards from me and wrote my name and address and national insurance number on the new cards with "Building and Civil Engineering" printed on them and gave them to me along with another card, the important green card, necessary for the change from one employer to another at that time. And that was that. The transition from agricultural worker to building site worker had taken place.

"John Carey and John Curry; not much difference in names between you two", said the clerk in the site office to me and the other man as we handed in our cards in the morning. We were both starting work with John Lawrence and Co. Curry was sent up the road by Carson to load lorries with the heavy squad, and I was sent in the opposite direction, to dig drains with MacEnroe, for which purpose I collected a shovel and a pickaxe, the tools of the trade, from the storehouse beside the office.

MacEnroe, a jocose type of man, asked me if I was any good at digging trenches for pipes. I told him truthfully that I had done a lot of digging in my time but I had never dug pipe tracks. "Ah, there is nothing to it, man", he said. "Just tear out the muck in big lumps and throw it well back."

The trenches, which were marked out with a line by the ganger, were about eighteen inches wide, and were excavated to various depts, depending on the height of the ground in relation to the ground floor level of the building the pipes were to serve. The higher the ground the deeper the trench. Seldom were they more than six feet deep or less than three. The three-foot-long fireclay pipes were laid down in the excavated trenches, always with a slight gradient towards the point where they linked up with the main sewer. Any able-bodied man who was used to digging could dig a pipe tract, and as long as he kept the sides of the cutting reasonably straight he could not go far wrong, but it took a fairly handy worker to "bottom"—finish off the bottom where the pipes were to lie and give it the right grade.

MacEnroe was right about the importance of throwing the newly-excavated earth well back. Piling it up too near the edge of the trench

118

could cause the sides to cave in because of the weight, especially in wet weather. Many a man lost his life in that way, or was badly injured, when a cutting for sewage pipes collapsed and crushed him.

All of MacEnroe's men were Irishmen and they were good men at digging trenches. Some wore wellingtons, others heavy hob-nailed boots, and they all had on either corduroy or moleskin trousers tied around below the knees with garters of strong twine. A man with his trouser legs tied in that way was said to be wearing "yorks". And they were very particular about keeping their shovels clean. Each had a sharpened sliver of wood for the purpose of scraping off any sticky earth that became attached to his shovel. The old men were tidier than the younger men. The older the man the more tidy a worker he seemed to be, and the more careful regarding his tools and the materials he worked with. Nowadays you will see tools lying around on building sites so caked with hardened concrete they can never be used again—good shovels and picks and barrows needlessly wasted, and as for the waste of building materials that goes on, it's a crying shame. The man, be he foreman or labourer, who did that kind of thing, or allowed it to be done in the old days on building sites, would not be long on the job. He would be sent down the road at short notice.

Another squad of about twenty men worked full-time digging out and concreting the foundations for the houses. All the digging on that site was done by men with picks and shovels. There was not a mechanical digger in the place. The earth from the founds was filled into wheelbarrows and taken out to be piled up into huge heaps nearby. Later it would come in useful for levelling off the lower areas around the site. A number of men worked at the cement mixer. Other men, wheeling barrows, took the concrete from the mixer into the founds where it was spread by Jimmy Lynch, the busiest man in the squad. Jimmy got paid one penny per hour more than the others, bringing his total hourly rate of pay up to two shillings and three pence. The man who operated the mixer got half an hour a day extra for starting up the machine in the morning and cleaning it in the evening—a quarter of an hour each time—thirteen pence a day.

Irishmen were considered to be good men working at a mixer. There was a story told that Sir Robert MacAlpine, the big contractor, shortly before his death, on passing on the recipes of success to his son, said: "Keep the big mixer going and keep Paddy behind it." Paddy was a good man behind the mixer. The day of the big mixer on building sites is gone now; concrete comes on to the job ready mixed, and so too is the day of the pick and shovel for digging founds and pipe tracks.

The ganger in charge of the concreting squad was Willie Quinn, a wiry little man who went rushing about in a donkey jacket twice too big for him and a big pair of wellington boots. "What like of a man is Quinn the ganger", asked a man who came looking for him one morning, having been told by Carson to go and start in Quinn's squad. "Oh, you can't miss him", said Paddy Gallagher. "He's a small man in a hurry, with a long jacket and a big pair of rubber boots." And that was an excellent description of Willie Quinn. Quinn was harassed by Carson, supposedly because he did not know his work. Not that Carson himself knew that much. Men like Dan Sweeney and Paddy Gallagher, who were the jointer and the pipe-layer in our squad, could teach the two of them.

The heavy gang, the squad Curry, the man who started the same day as I did, was assigned to, worked all over the place, loading and unloading, and moving anything that required to be moved. They were not a big squad of men in number, no more than seven or eight of them altogether. Their ganger, Guy Nimmo, a Scotsman, was regarded as a decent man to work under. It was said that the man who could not get on with Guy would not get on with any man. But no matter how decent the man himself was I still would not have liked to work in his squad. It was not for nothing they were called the heavy gang. And often we were called upon to give them a helping hand. Always on wet days when we were in the hut, sheltering from the rain, that was when the influx of lorries was sure to come laden with cement, and slabs, and lintels and kerbstones, or with pipes for the drains, or tiles or timber for the roofs, or steel for shuttering, you name it, one or more lorryloads of it was sure to arrive every wet day—by design, some said. And then Carson would come into the hut, and it was, "you and you, and you, get out and help unload them lorries." And rain or no rain, out we had to go, and I can tell you that it was not blessing him or the lorries we used to be. From then on, until the last day ever I worked on a construction site, the unloading of lorries in the rain remained my pet hate.

The tradesmen and their labourers did not sit in the same hut as we did to take their tea or shelter from the rain. They all had quarters to themselves. It could be said that the rules of apartheid existed. And they existed in more ways than one. They existed between the Scots and the Irish, and more so between the supporters of Celtic and

Rangers. Even when in the same hut, those of different race and persuasion tended to keep apart form each other. The two Poles in our hut seemed to hit it off better with the Irish than with the Scots. Between themselves they spoke in their own language and some said that it was talking about the rest of us they used to be. But I do not think that was correct. I think they had every right to converse together in their own tongue, which came easy and natural to them. And what if they did talk about us sometimes, maybe we deserved it.

One of them taught me several words in Polish. The Polish for window, he told me, was "okno", and for eye it was "oko" the same bar one letter. Shovel was "vobatha" and pickaxe was "bake". In the end I was able to say a few short sentences in Polish, such as "hand me the shovel", or "did you see my pickaxe".

We were allowed two tea breaks every day; the first, a short one of about ten minutes at nine in the morning, and the main break of half an hour at midday. As soon as the whistle blew for "tea up" every man headed as fast as he could for the hut known as the canteen, where the cans of water boiled on the big charcoal fire. Here the nipper held sway; not a boy but a cheeky middle-aged little tyke of a man who had the nickname "Dry Balls". How he got that name I do not know, but he had it and he did not like it. It was better not to say it in his hearing. His job was to keep the huts reasonably tidy and to have the cans boiling at the right times. But they were not always boiling when they should have been; often, many of them were far from it. One way to encourage Dry Balls to have your can boiling was to give him an odd shilling for himself on the quiet, and that was far more effective than arguing with him or abusing him like some men did. And the same Dry Balls was able to give as good as he got in an abusive argument.

Every man on the site drank his tea from a smoke-blackened tin can. Those cans could be bought in any hardware shop and in most newsagents, and if a man came on to the job without one he would not be without one for long as there were always spares lying about the huts. A can that had been in use for some time made a good brew of tea, tasting better than from a teapot. And as those cans boiled over the big fire in Springboig, I noticed some men break off half a match stick and throw it into the water; the tea did not have such a smoky taste, they said, when a small bit of wood was boiled in it. Every man knew his own can and it would not be good for any young fellow who tried taking the wrong one. Many a good drink of tea I enjoyed from the black tin cans on the building sites.

The storeman, the man in charge of tools and materials was like the nipper, another man with an easy job and a contrary manner. He was a hard man to get anything out of; no use going to him looking for as much as a nail without a line from the foreman. He once chased me because, having mislaid my shovel (or maybe some man took it when I wasn't looking), I went into the store and took another while he was in the lavatory across the way. He returned just as I was going off with it and he made me leave it back again. When I came a short while later with the necessary prescription he let me have the tool, albeit in a reluctant sort of way, as if he would have preferred not to give it. I suppose he had to be exact, otherwise things could go missing, but I an inclined to think he was a bit more exact and officious than he needed to be.

MacEnroe was not a bad old codger for a ganger. Navvy gangers were seldom noted for their fairness or for their leniency towards the workers and maybe he was a bit too easy for his job. He was reduced to the ranks after that scheme was completed, and when I came across him again a few years later, at Thornliebank, he was down in the trench with a pick and shovel, tearing it out and throwing it up like the rest of them. His health deteriorated after that and he died in the early fifties while still a few years off retiring age.

As Christmas drew near the home sickness came on me again and I sailed once more from the Broomielaw to Dublin. But unlike the previous year we had a rough night at sea. I was sea-sick for the first and only time in my life, a thoroughly unpleasant experience, and that is putting it mildly. We should have been in Dublin at eight o'clock in the morning but it was one in the afternoon before we got in and we were lucky we ever got there. It was a bad night going down the Irish Sea. A few years afterwards the Stranraer-Belfast boat, the "Princess Victoria", got lost in daylight on the shorter crossing with the loss of over a hundred and fifty lives. I remember the day well. But our time was not up, we made Dublin safely, five hours late.

Four others from the Belmullet district were on the boat that night, two sisters from down Pollathomas way and a young couple from Binghamstown. We were about four hours late for the Ballina train, so we got a train to Castlebar instead. At least it would take us nearer home, we reasoned. Having got that far, we were standing discussing what would be the best thing for us to do—stay in Castlebar overnight and get the bus to Ballina in the morning, or hire private transport to Belmullet—when we were approached by a local hackney driver. Either he had overheard us talking or someone had told him about us; whatever it was he knew we wanted to get to Belmullet and he offered to take us there for twelve shillings each. I suggested to him that he deliver us to our homes for the twelve shillings and he agreed. The man had let himself in for more than he realised. To drive from Pollathomas to Binghamstown and then to Morahan was in itself a journey over half as long as from Castlebar to Belmullet. He did not know the layout of the Belmullet district or that it was such a far-flung place. He knew better before he had finished, and I, the one responsible for stricking the bargain, and the last to be let off, suffered the edge of his tongue so much I gave him an extra half-crown to pacify him. Then he said I wasn't a bad lad after all. And all the time the rain kept lashing down as it so often does in the west of Ireland.

My mother was sitting by the fire knitting when I walked in the door. The big turf fire in the open hearth made the kitchen delightfully warm and cosy and I was glad to be home. After something to eat I walked along the road back to Anthony Walsh's house. The rain had stopped at last but it was windy and cold outside, colder than I had felt it in Scotland, and with the biting wind of open seaside places that can go right through a person.

When I came to Anthony's door I did not knock but lifted the latch and walked in. That was the way in that part of the world, people never bothered to knock when they came to a neighbour's house. My father and Pack Gaughan were there with Anthony and his aged mother, Biddy, and them all centred around the fire conversing about some matter of local interest. The fire was always the focus point in every house before television came; had been, I believe, for thousands of years, and everybody always sat more or less facing it. I was half way up the floor before they saw me.

Anthony had spent a number of years in Glasgow shortly after the First World War, and he was interested in hearing news about it. He was surprised when I told him that the whole area between Giffnock and Newton Mearns was all built over with houses. "My God", he said, (that was an expression he had) "when I was there, there was miles and miles of wide open country between Giffnock and Newton Mearns."

It was late when the three of us, Pack, my father and myself, came over to our house. Pack's wife Biddy was there along with their son Paddy. Mary Jo had been to their house to tell them I was home and they had come in to see me. I took out some bottles of Guinness that I bought on the way and we drank them there beside the fire. Pack, after some egging on, sang his favourite song, the patriot song "John Mitchell"—about the true-born Irishman who would sooner die for freedom than live in slavery. Because of his fight for freedom in Ireland he was shipped off as a convict to Van Diemans Land (Tasmania) from which he afterwards escaped and made his way to America, where strange to relate, though the song did not say so, he became a strong supporter of slavery during the civil war in which my great-grandfather fought on the side of freedom. The freedom of the blacks in America cannot have meant the same to that John Mitchell as did the freedom of Ireland. Like many a man he was a bit of a contradiction.

The next couple of weeks passed quickly, too quickly, and then it was time for me to hit the road again, back to Scotland. More by accident than by design I had as company with me on the return journey two girls: one was from Tipp, the other from Faulmore. They too had been home from Scotland for Christmas and like myself they had experienced a rough crossing on the Dublin boat. Talking about it on the bus to Ballina we decided that it might be a good idea for us to go back the Belfast way as it was a much shorter sea voyage. The Belfast boat completed the run to Glasgow in seven hours—nine at the longest. The Dublin boat took sixteen hours even on a good night. So our plan was that we would carry on by bus to Sligo, get the train there for Belfast, and cross to Glasgow on the Belfast boat.

But our plan misfired. We did not see Belfast that night. The connections did not connect; not for us anyhow, for when we got to Sligo it was to find the Belfast train had departed, and all we could do then was to stay the night there. We got ourselves fixed up with bed and breakfast accommodation and then I asked the two women if they would like to come out with me for a drink. They declined the invitation; they did not like going into pubs, they said. One of them went one further in her dislikes; she did not like the way men went into pubs, she said. I never saw much wrong with the way men, or for that matter women either, went into pubs. It's the state they can get themselves into when they are in the pub, and the way they can be coming out to them—that was the part of it I never liked.

I went into the pub in Sligo on my own that evening, and there I got into conversation with the barman. I mentioned to him I was after coming from Belmullet. "What you are drinking came from Belmullet too", said he, drawing my attention to the words on the label of the Guinness bottle: "Bottled by McIntyre's Stores Belmullet". McIntyre's were one of the biggest business concerns in the west of Ireland at that time. So strong and affluent were they I never thought then I would see the day they would go into liquidation. But as Ned Kelly said before they hanged him, "such is life". The world is full of ups and downs; it is changing the whole time and nobody can tell what the future has in store.

We got to Belfast the following day. While passing through Northern Ireland I remember noticing the large number of hens at the farm houses. Poultry farming must have been very popular in the North at that time. There must have been well over a hundred hens at many of the houses, maybe a couple of hundred.

On the boat I again visited the public bar on my own; I did not bother asking my two female fellow-travellers to come this time. They would not have come, and just as well, for I do not think they would have liked the man I struck up company with there. But to me he was an interesting man, an old fellow of about seventy who had travelled all over Ireland and most of Scotland. He was a tinker and like all tinkers he had been around a bit. He knew Belmullet and had camped at Fanny's Hill, a few miles out of the town along the Ballina road. He had many stories to tell about his travels. Amongst other things he told me that Seán MacEoin, the far-famed blacksmith of Ballinalee in Longford, who besides being a blacksmith had also been a famous freedom fighter, an army general, and a government minister, though not all at the same time, had often shod ponies for him. And he spoke very well of MacEoin. "A decent man", he said, "he would do as much for a travelling man as he would for any man." He was a decent enough man himself too. He did not shirk his turn when it was time for him to buy a drink and I never felt the time passing listening to his crack. He might not have been much to look at, nor might folk of his calling have had much of a reputation, but to quote Robert Burns, "a man is a man for all that". I say, take a man the way you find him.

It was still dark when we came off at the Broomielaw. The two girls went their way and I went mine. They had been an aloof and stand-offish pair on the journey, except when they wanted something done for them like lugging suitcases around, then they could be nice enough. The buses and trams were crowded with people on their way to work—a big change from that time of the morning around home: few if any in the town of Belmullet would be up and about at half past six of a cold January morning. They would only have their second sleep made by then and another good sleep still ahead of them. And I had not slept at all.

By the time I reached Hospital Street the other lodgers had left for their work and the house was quiet and silent. I went to bed and was soon fast asleep. I awoke when Mrs Hannigan came into the room with tea on a tray for me, and for a moment I did not know right where I was. I had been dreaming about home, a mixed up thing, as dreams so often are, in which I thought Seán MacEoin was shoeing horses below in Pat Walsh's forge, and then again I thought it was Martin Gaughan that was doing it. I was surprised to see that it was already early afternoon; I had slept longer than I thought I had. I got up, washed and shaved, and spent the rest of the evening in the George Picture House in Crown Street.

Heavy snow fell and lay on the ground for about two weeks or more with the result there was little outside work could be done in that time. Some had gloomy forecasts that it was going to be like 1947, two years before which was the worst in living memory and all the building sites closed down, but it did not turn out that bad. The big pay off we were afraid of never came, though it must have cost the contractor a lot to keep us on. We spent a lot of the time in huts. Some men played cards, some talked about football or betting, or told stories about their past experiences on other jobs. I enjoyed listening to them. Jimmy Lynch, the concrete spreader, was a good story-teller. He was an ex-Free State army man, and an ex-boxer. He was an ex-many things if it was true for himself. Jimmy could spin the yarns. The MacGowan brothers from Leitrim were good crack too, the three of them: Paddy, Jimmy and Phil. They were small roundish-built fellows, good talkers, and good friends to have on one's side, but I would not like to have them as enemies. They could fight as well as talk. But the daddy of them all was an old Mayo man, Mick Cafferkey, or "McCafferty", as some called him, and he was seventy-five if he was a day. For well over fifty years he had worked, or "wrought", to use the navvy expression (and he had all the navvy words), on big construction jobs up and down Britain, and he was only with Lawrence because he was "no good for anything else now". He had the most spontaneous flow of talk—I think he was the most fluent man I ever heard and I have heard lawyers and politicians and may a one; but that old working man had a command of words the like of which I have never heard. And he could spout them out so fast I don't know how his mouth kept up with his brain or vice versa. He claimed he had a nephew a TD in Ireland, "and it was from his old uncle Mick he took the gift of the gab". Often I have been thinking that if old Mick Cafferkey's talk had been taken down and published it would have made interesting reading.

I became good friends with Denis Casey from County Monaghan, and together we used to go to the Irish dancing which was held at that time in some place in Glasgow every night of the week, and in several places on Sunday nights. The Irish political party, Fianna Fáil, had a strong-going branch here and they ran dancing to boost their coffers every Sunday night in an old hall in Clydeferry Street, patronised by their Donegal-Irish supporters, and by others like me who were not supporters, but who went, nonetheless, for the entertainment. Frank O'Neill and his Cill Dara Club had their dances in Errol Street in the south side. Some enterprising person, or persons, held what passed for dancing in a place called the Cuba in Paisley Road West, and that was the rowdy place. It was entered by ascending a steep flight of stairs, both winding and narrow, and it wasn't into heaven you were going when you went up those stairs and into the Cuba. It was most times overcrowded and uncomfortably stuffy, and it was hell when the fights started, because with the crush of people there wasn't room to swing a cat. One fellow I knew, Joe Burke, got flung down the stairs to his death, and the poor lad had not been involved in the trouble at all. He was at the top of the stairs about to come in when he was violently pushed in the melee and went over the banister.

An equally enterprising woman by the name of Eileen Boyce held dances in a basement in Stobcross Street; you had to go down the stairs to get into that one; while garrulous old Frank Conemey had his noisy unruly hoolies in Bishop Street. The Catholic Church too was in on the act. St Luke's in the Gorbals, St Margaret's in Kinning Park, and St Simon's in Partick, were only a few of the parochial venues where Irish jigging flourished on certain nights, providing, I believe, a nice addition to parish funds, and under the fatherly eye of the parish priest or one of his curates. One thing I will say for the parish halls, they were better run than the other dives, and that was easy for them.

The bands, like the halls, left much to be desired. Fellows who wheeled barrows of concrete or dug out pipe tracks by day earned an extra few bob on the side pulling an old box mellodian or rasping at an old fiddle by night. That was the kind of bands they had. They made noise, plenty of noise; they had amplifiers in the halls—loud speakers—to enable them to make up in volume for what they lacked in skill.

The Irish dances in Glasgow, plenty and all as they were, were only poor comparison to the dances at home. For one thing, they only lasted about two or three hours—not much compared to the all night until morning dos in Ireland. People had to be up early in the morning for their work, so everything ended about eleven o'clock. Some tried to make up for this by starting proceedings early in the evening but that did not work out. I don't think I ever saw a dance get going in the right swing before nine o'clock, and it's an unnatural thing in summertime, in the light evenings—a crowd of young people within in an old hall dancing, and the sun shining outside. Far better go to the park: and that was what we often done on fine evenings; we went up to Queen's Park and lay there.

So on the whole the dances were nothing to write home about, but they were places for meeting the girls, the pub at that time being an almost male domain. If you had a girlfriend the chances were you met her at the dancing, and the better a fellow was as a dancer, the better his chances with the young ladies. Having met and hit it off together the usual routine of a courting couple was to go to a dance or to the pictures one or more nights a week, that is if they had the money to get in, which was a thing they did not always have. Cinemas abounded, yet so popular was film-going every one of them had two queues outside it every night for six nights of the week (they did not open on Sundays)—a big queue for the stalls and a smaller queue for the balcony. About nine o'clock everybody usually got in for the last showing of the big film. If there weren't seats they let them stand at the back or in the aisles unless it was very crowded altogether. Only on very rare occasions did people fail to get in at that time of the evening.

I hardly every went to a pub except on Saturday nights, and then only for an hour or so before closing time; but I went most Saturday nights and I am the same way yet. Nearly every man I knew in those days who was half a man at all took a few drinks either on Friday or Saturday night, some on both nights. All public houses closed at nine-thirty and they had their clocks set about ten minutes fast, so as to be sure they would not be late in closing. Men drank to beat the clock and coming near closing time it was chaos with all the pushing and shouting, trying to draw the attentions of the bar tenders, and guzzling down drink like if there was no tomorrow. And anybody who knows anything about drinking knows what happens when it's taken too fast.

Every time an extension of opening hours was petitioned for it was vigorously opposed by certain elements of the public, very often people who had never been inside a public house in their lives. They might not have liked what they saw when men came out at closing time, stone clobbered, and they could not be blamed for not liking it; but one sure way to make people drink it up fast and thereby get drunk all the more is to have short drinking hours. Shorter hours serves to increase drunkenness, not to decrease it: that is a proven fact. There are some, and always were, and I suppose always will be, who would have all the public houses closed down altogether if they got their way. Others think a pub is all right anywhere as long as it is not too near to where they live. I think a pub is all right anywhere as long as it is used the right way. As my mother used to say "too much of anything is good for nothing". I have been enjoying a few pints of beer at the weekends for a long time now, and I hope to go on doing so for a while yet.

CHAPTER FIFTEEN

A Navvy's Life

OUT AT SPRINGBOIG some of the men were becoming restless. They talked a lot about other sites where there were good hours and good money. Good hours meant long hours—plenty of overtime to swell up the pay packet. They talked about jobs where the men were working seven twelve-hour shifts every week—from eight in the morning until eight at night. We finished at four-thirty every day during the week and twelve on Saturdays. But we worked every Sunday. The Sunday shift with double time was as good as two other days, but even so we came out with only seven pounds a week. Up in the north, on the hydro-electric schemes, men were earning twice that and more.

Lawrence's were about as good a building firm to work for as there was around Glasgow. We had a guaranteed forty-four-hour week, which meant we were sure of eight-hours pay for every day throughout the week and four hours on Saturday. We got that no matter how the weather was; whether it was fit to work out in it or not. Most construction firms only guaranteed their men a thirty-two-hour week, meaning in practice they only got half an hour for every hour they were rained off. Thirty-two-hours pay was no good for a week.

On the hydro schemes was where the good money could be made, working in the tunnels. The "tunnel tigers" as they were called, came down at the weekends, all rough and scruffy, and badly in need of a bath, but with plenty of money in their pockets. They would explain, to let us know the hardy breed of men they were, about the terrible conditions they endured. They would talk about the horse work, toiling in the compressed air, deep down in the bowels of the earth and far from the light of day, working long twelve- and fourteen-hour shifts, shovelling like mad, or blasting out rock, or using drills or jack hammers, or wearing thigh-length rubber boots, deep in concrete or in mud, and with a tyrant of a ganger, or section foreman, bellowing, urging them to get on with the work. And it was mostly true. No wonder those men became prematurely old and died before their time.

And always they had the pay slips to show, to prove the big money they were earning—twelve and fourteen pounds a week clear. The Irishmen were noted for flashing the pay-slips. A pay envelope showing a high figure of money for a week's work was a thing to keep for showing in pubs in order to impress people. A Pole was reputed to have said: "The Irishman throws away the money and keeps the empty packet, the Pole keeps the money and throws away the empty packet." He might never have said it, but there was a lot of truth in it, for all too often that was what happened.

By April, many of the younger men who had been on the Springboig site since the previous summer had departed elsewhere. The old ones did not go; they would be there until the job was finished, unless they got paid off before that. I missed the lads who went away and although others came in their place, it was not the same. I was getting restless myself by then. My mate Casey, the Monaghan man, was no longer there; he had gone to work for Wimpey on the building of the new oil refinery at Grangemouth.

One day, a fellow by the name of Connor, a fine big strapping Donegal man of rather wild and unpredictable manner who was working beside me in the trench, suddenly jumped up on to the bank, and swinging his shovel around three or four times, something in the way of one throwing a stone from a sling, flung it away from him as far as he could, whilst mouthing a few obscenities at the same time. "What's the matter with you, Connor?" I asked. "I'm digging no more on this fucking old job, that's what's the matter", said he. "I'm away to jack", meaning he was packing it in. And with that he went off, down to the office.

I was not long behind Connor. I jacked too. One of the older men asked me did I have any job in mind to go to. He said something about anyone being silly enough to do what they saw "that mad buggar Connor" doing. But I wasn't just copying Connor. I had the notion in my head for a while; it was just that his action triggered it off; only for that I might have stayed a bit longer.

Married men with homes and families could not jack up their jobs and go looking for somewhere else to work whenever they felt like it as easy as single men with no cares or responsibilities could, and some of them took a poor view to the pointless moving about from one site to another that went on amongst the young fellows. "If they were here before the war they would be glad to have a job to stay on", they would say.

With my cards in my pocket I set out to look for another building site to labour on, a not very difficult task at that particular time. The years immediately following the war saw the greatest house construction programme under way that ever was known in Britain, and the west of Scotland got its share of the building. No matter where you went, for miles into the country in every direction from Glasgow, houses were going up by the thousand. Green fields were being torn up and ravished as a network of roads were being laid, while all around sprang up houses, houses and more houses. Those were the years when the vast sprawling estates were built: Easterhouse, Drumchapel, Pollok, and many many more. They were going to build houses for everybody and transplant the towns out into the open country. They tore up whole communities as well as whole countrysides and created as many problems as they solved, but that is another story.

A common feature to be seen on those post-war housing projects were the droves of city and townsmen sent out to work on them from the labour exchange, men who were in no way suitable for that type of work. Some of them had not worked for years, some had never done a stroke of work in their lives, and did not intend to if they could get away with it. Many were unemployable. It was ludicrous sending men like that out to do strenuous labouring work on construction sites. Most had little heart for the work: all they wanted was to get back on the dole and this they invariably attained after a few weeks when they were given their cards and sent back to where they came from, only to be replaced the following week by a similar useless batch. With so many of those fellows coming and going and serving no useful purpose, an Irishman had no problem in getting put to work when he came on to a site, because Irishmen, almost without exception, were known to be good workmen.

At the first site where I called looking for work the day I left Lawrence's, the foreman said: "Come out in the morning, I'm getting rid of three or four of them latchicoes from the buroo this evening." He must have expected me to do as much work as the three of them, or four of them, whichever it was. And if he did itself that would be no bother to me. My grandmother would have done as much as any six of them.

132

I stuck with the new job for a month or so. It was constructing prefabricated houses (prefabs) we were, and it was the ideal place for any man looking for long hours. By the time I got in at night it was near time to go to bed, and that seven days a week. The job was rushed; they wanted the prefabs put up within a certain limit of time. The ganger was a gruff, outsized west of Ireland man, and he had with him an assortment of brothers, brothers-in-law and other relations who formed an inner circle. This crowd had been sent up from England by the firm and each of them was getting a lodging allowance giving them a good extra in their pay packets along with all the overtime. Another man working there, and a very nice man, was Mick Heraghty from the borders of Mayo and Galway, and we became good friends.

I got fed up with the job as I had no time at all to myself and they did not want you if you were not prepared to work all the hours of the day. Those, as far as I know, were the last prefabs to be put up around Glasgow. I jacked again, and then I started with Wimpey in Lambhill.

At the fair in the middle of July I was off work for a week. The annual summer holiday break only lasted a week in those days compared to a fortnight later on and almost all works of every kind were shut down for the duration. Looking back on it now I think that was one of the happiest and most carefree weeks of my life. I was young and I was free, and it was a marvellous thing to be able to stay in bed sleeping in the morning instead of getting up early for work. It was about midday every day before I got dressed either in my blue suit or in my sports jacket and flannels, and in the evening I would surely go over to the shows on Glasgow Green. On my way back I would go into the Wheatsheaf in Crown Street where I would meet Heraghty, or Tommy Joyce, another Galway man, or some of the Belmullet men, maybe Mick Keane or Mick Crean or Paddy Keane. I would end up the night at the pictures or at one of the Irish dance halls. I thought that was a marvellous way to spend the time and that no man could wish for a better holiday or a nicer way of life.

I enjoyed the shows on the Green at the fair time. They were worth going to then, something that could not be said for them in later years. There was a boxing booth where for two shillings could be seen four fights, each fight lasting four rounds and I considered that good value for money. Some good professional boxers fought there, including

Willie White the welter-weight champion of Scotland, light-weight champion Don MacTaggart, and Pat McCoy from Ireland. Four pounds was the prize money for any man who went the distance with any of them, and there was no shortage of ex-boxers, and would-be boxers, and chancers, to take them on. We loved to see McCoy, the Irishman, fight, and all the Irish lads cheered him on, whether he deserved it or not. He was only a short little fellow, but sturdily built and a born scrapper. He and a Murphy man from Bridgeton fought three times that week, and it was pronounced a draw every time, so evenly matched they were. Murphy was taller than McCoy but I would not say he was as experienced.

Amongst the other attractions on offer as part of the fun of the fair on Glasgow Green was a booth where "young ladies" took off their clothes for the benefit of the audience, admission also two shillings. The matronly broad-hipped woman who stood outside before each show calling on all who were passing to step inside and savour the delights within kept repeating the same words over and over again, so often did she say them the children had them by heart and went around repeating them. "Gentlemen come in. And when you will see those ladies remove their garments one by one, and stand naked before you, wearing nothing in the world but a smile, if it does not stir you on the inside, you should come out and go to see your doctor without delay."

The strippers themselves, two generously-proportioned ladies, buxom and well painted, stood beside her as she spoke, wriggling their bodies in tune with the gramophone music in the background. I went in there once, more from curiosity than anything else, and I did not see much. I could have saved my two shillings for better use had I heeded a man who was after coming out: "It's a cheat", he said. And he was right there.

It was a cheat all right. All the stripping that took place in there was done behind a semi-transparent curtain, and all the goggle-eyed punters, who included a mixture of women, got to see for their money was the shadow of arms being raised as a jumper and bra came off, and legs being kicked up as knickers were removed, and the garments brandished about at arms length. And then the show was over, and the woman explained to us that they had done all the law allowed— "the law forbids any more to be shown". Then they went outside and the wriggling and the reciting started all over again.

I never went in there again. Nor did I go near the doctor because it had not turned me on. I got a ticking off from the priest in St Luke's when I told him about it in Confession. "Keep away from such dangerous occasions of sin", he warned me. God help the poor man's sense; he did not know at all. I saw more to tickle the sex buds when women and girls lifted up their petticoats above their thighs and sometimes above their waists to cross the ferry at home.

At Lambhill I was a bricklayer's labourer carrying the hod. The hod, for anyone who does not know, was a V-shaped wooden box for carrying bricks and mortar on the shoulders of the bearer. This box had a handle sticking down out of it, about the same in length and thickness as the handle of an average spade. When the box rested on the shoulder the handle came down against the bearer's side, much the same as a soldier holds his rifle when standing to attention. Some men carried the hod for years, labouring to the brickies and to the plasters, until they became all slewed to one side with a shoulder up and a shoulder down and you would know they were hod carriers from a mile away. And it wouldn't have been too bad if you only had to carry the damn thing while moving about on the ground, but you were expected to climb ladders all day with it. Talk about a beast of burden. The ass carrying the *bardógs* of turf on his back had an easier job than a hod carrier. But I soon left them and their hod carrying to it.

It was in a pub in Crown Street on a Friday night I was told about the new building scheme that was started up near Rutherglen—the Spittal scheme it was called. R.W. Stewart, "a good firm", were the contractors; they were starting men there, and there was "good hours on the job", the man who told me said. So I decided to pack in with Wimpey and try Stewart. As soon as I arrived on the job next morning the first thing I done was to ask at the office for my cards and lying time. I had to hang around waiting for a while; it was around ten o'clock before they had them ready for me. I got the bus to Rutherglen, came off in the main street, and following directions from someone I asked I walked up Mill Street. I walked half a mile or so before I came in sight of the new building work and when I saw the signboards with Stewart's name on them I knew then that I was in the right place.

The land the scheme was being built on had formerly been the Spittal Farm and the old farm house was being used as a site office. When I went up to the foreman who was standing in the door of the farm house and asked him the usual question, "any chance of the start?" he replied at once, "Yes, come out and start on Monday." I was walking away, well pleased, when he called me back. Would I like to start right now, by any chance, he asked. When I said I would like that, he told me to go down and give a helping hand to two men who were digging a hole by the roadside. And he told me I could work that afternoon and the next day, Sunday, if I wanted. "We are working every weekend", he said.

I had packed up in one place at ten o'clock that Saturday and started within the hour on another job ten miles away. I was doing fine.

Bob Stewart was the managing director of R.W. Stewart & Co. Bob was a man of simple tastes and manners who dressed in a well-worn grey suit and smoked a clay pipe, one of the few men I ever saw smoking a clay pipe in Scotland. Other directors in the firm were William Smith, Andrew Braidwood and Joseph Cobley. They were all said to be Free Masons, but be that as it may, they were decent enough towards their workers: as long as a man did a fair day's work he had nothing to fear from any of them.

I was put on the the concreting of the founds the week after I started with Stewart. We had no cement mixer. The concrete was all mixed by hand—turning on the board they called it, as we had a flooring of boards under us where we worked, turning and mixing concrete with shovels. It was good work for keeping men warm in cold weather. Eight of us worked full time on the board: some barrowing on gravel and sand and throwing on the bag of cement needed for every batch; two men turning it over dry and two others turning it over wet, after water had been added from a hose. The men who did the wheeling into the founds never worked on the board; wheeling barrows was their job and that was all they done. Tommy Forrest was the ganger. Tommy was all right, a bit of a hot head be times, but a good man to work under.

The ganger in charge of the excavation work was Hughie McCann, an elderly man who walked with a limp. That was how he got his nickname, "Hopalong Cassidy". But Hughie did not like the name, and I would not like to have been the one to call it to him in his presence. There were a lot of things he did not like and a lot of people who did not like him. He had been with Stewart for a long time, ever since he came to the country as a young man. Men said he was made a ganger because, though a conscientious and handy worker, labouring came difficult to him on account of his bad leg. It was a Mayo man, Patsy Togher, who had been a ganger with Stewart in the nineteen-twenties, made McCann what he was. Patsy took him under his wing and taught him all the tricks of the trade—how to take levels and so on—and after some years when Togher went away to another firm McCann succeeded him as ganger. In the bad old days of the thirties Togher came back and he was put to work under McCann who turned out to be a foul man to him, gave him all the hard and dirty jobs to do, and made it so bad for him that he soon left again.

One thing more than anything else that sticks in my memory about Hughie McCann was how fastidious and tidy he was, and how he always kept his working boots clean and polished; no matter what state they were in going home at night he came out next morning with them shining immaculate. And he was that way in everything: tidy, precise, exact, and punctual. All day long he would be around where the men were working, giving instructions and directions, telling them to do this thing one way and that thing another way, making sure everything was right, down to the smallest detail. Working under a man like that could make the day seem very long.

One man who worked for a short time with McCann asked him one day if he was an Orangeman. "Not at all", replied Hughie, taken aback at being asked such a thing: "I am a Catholic." And so he was, and a very practising one too, I believe. "You would not make a good fucking Orangeman", retorted the other. "A good Orangeman goes for a walk at least once a year—on the twelfth of July—but you never seem to take a walk." "I don't like that kind of talk", said McCann angrily, and his under lip shot out, a bad sign. "Well, I don't like the way you stand over me all day showing me how to dig out a bit of old fucking muck." And the man put on his jacket and went to collect his cards.

We were not under McCann, and we were glad of that. Tommy Forrest was our ganger at the concreting. McCann tried a few times to interfere, came nosying around, offering unsolicited advice, but he never carried it too far. If he thought Tommy was becoming annoyed with him he went away. Tommy had the reputation of being a man who would put in a blow as quick as he would speak, but he was a straight man, none of the fly man about him.

Duncan Glen, the general foreman, the man who started me that

Saturday, was what we called a Christian. I suppose we were all Christians really only Duncan was a much stricter Christian than the rest of us. He belonged to some kind of a sect (when I heard them saying it first I thought it was sex they were talking about). He did not drink or smoke, or use swear words, and it was said he did not listen to the radio on Sundays. They said he believed that the end of the world was close at hand, but if he did, he did not act like if it was, not where the work was concerned anyhow. End of the world or no end of the world, Duncan liked to see the work getting done. But having said that it is only fair to say too that he was not a man who would wrong or harm anybody. He was good as a foreman.

Two men who worked side by side with me shovelling on the board were Eddie O'Boyle and Hugh Brennan, one a Mayo man, the other a Tyrone man. Both were in late middle age and both were bachelors but that was not the main reason why they impressed me. It was because they were so well read for working men. Through using public libraries and buying second-hand books at the Barrows, they had gained a vast amount of knowledge about history, and they had good memories. Both were fond of an argument, maybe sometimes too much so. Soon I was going to the library too, a practice I started through listening to them. Very few Irish people in Glasgow have, to my knowledge, used public libraries to much of an extent, and I think that is a great pity for not only does reading help cultivate the mind, a good book can be an interesting pastime and costs nothing to borrow. I have not been able to remember the things I read as good as those two did, or anything like it, nor can I make my point as well as they could. They were two good old workers and even when they were arguing like hell about who did what in the French Revolution or something else, they carried on working at the same time. Forrest said better to let them be because the more they argued the better they worked. John Lally said it was all "codology" they talked, but it was not. They knew what they were talking about and I found them to be both entertaining and instructive to listen to. They had read a lot and had been around for a long time.

O'Boyle in his youth had been active in the Sinn Féin movement in Mayo and had taken part in the Civil War on the anti-treaty side. Soon after that he left Ireland and never went back, not even for a holiday. In Scotland, through his experiences, and, I believe, through his readings, his leanings went more and more to the left until by the time I knew him he was an out and out communist and atheist. Some

138

of his own countrymen did not have much time for him because of his anti-religious views, but I believe he was sincere in them, and although I did not agree with him I respected his right to adhere to his convictions.

Brennan had been around Glasgow for a long number of years, over forty years in all, and he had always been keenly interested in politics without taking an active part in them. He told me that in the early years of the century he often went every night of the week to listen to the debates that then took place in Glasgow Green, and to the speeches of the pioneers of the labour movement—Keir Hardie and others. He had a great regard for John MacLean, the Scottish Socialist Republican agitator who died in 1923 at the age of forty-four years, worn out by imprisonment and overwork. That was one thing Brennan and O'Boyle were agreed upon, that MacLean was a great man and a true martyr for the cause of the workers.

Brennan had worked down the pits for most of his life. He was a brusher, he told me. I said he must have worn down many a scrubbing brush in his time. He turned on me in anger. "If you had to do it you would know", he snapped. A brusher's work, it seems, did not involve sweeping out the place. It had to do with removing substances not belonging to the coal seam, such as rock and shale, and also propping up the place so that the colliers could work in comparative safety. It was a responsible job and no wonder he got annoyed with me taking the mickey, talking about sweeping with brushes.

Peter Hogg was another bachelor. He was not as old as Brennan or O'Boyle but a confirmed bachelor just the same, and whereas they both had houses of their own Peter was a "modeller"—he lived in the public lodging house, the Tontine, near Glasgow Cross. Peter was not a man who would break any harness working; with him it was easy and slow and constant the whole time. He never rushed it, but he would never be caught idle; he had a pace and a rhythm, the pattern of which he never broke. And beyond any man I ever knew he showed no awareness of either the heat or the cold. No matter how warm the day was it made no difference to Peter; when the rest of us threw off our shirts he left on his jacket. We used to joke that maybe it was glued to him. When the winter came, and the frost and snow, and with the cold biting winds blowing in from the Fenwick Moors, on days when, as Eddie O'Boyle said, it would freeze the nose of a brass monkey, then we came out in the mornings muffled up with scarves and overcoats. But not "Peter the Navvy". He showed up with the same outfit on as he had in summer, no overcoat, no pullover, and the shirt unbuttoned almost to the waist. The man gave no indication of feeling either the summer's heat or the winter's cold. He was a phenomenon. Hugh Brennan said it could be that his mind had complete control over his body. "The body feels what the mind suggests", said Hughie. "Start talking to people about lice and they will feel itchy, mention about a bad cold going around and they will start sniffling."

McCann's wife opened a dairy in Hillhead and so eager was Hughie to promote the family business he started selling eggs to the workers on the site. Every morning he came limping up the road carrying a big basket of eggs with him. They were good eggs by all accounts and good they should have been; he was charging dear enough for them. I never bought any of his eggs—why should I? I was paying the landlady and getting plenty to eat from her so there was no need for me to go buying eggs from McCann.

Bob Stewart found out about the egg selling on the job and he put an end to it, and also to the sideline operated by another fellow, one of the brickies' labourers, who, encouraged by McCann's example and success with the eggs (or maybe on his own initiative), took in smoked herring to sell on certain days of the week. For this his mates nicknamed him "Kipper". They said his wife worked in a fish-mongers and that she got the herring cheap. So that was two of them whose little private enterprises were hit on the head by the contractor.

When the frosts came the concreting was temporarily suspended and then we were out digging trenches for pipes the same as I had been doing with John Lawrence. The pipelayer was Johnny Curran. Johnny was another bachelor (there was a lot more bachelors around in those days), and like Peter Hogg he was never a man to rush things. He took time and pains with everything he did, making sure his work was thorough. "If a job is worth doing, it's worth doing right"; that was his motto, and he lived up to it. He sold me a wrist watch for thirty shillings. A pocket watch would suit him better, he said, because there was too much electricity in his blood and it made the watch go too fast. The electricity never made Johnny himself go too fast, whatever about the watch. I never did get that watch to go with any satisfaction.

Like a good many others I knew on the construction jobs, little Johnny Bonar, the diminutive man who jointed the pipes, had his nickname—"Billy the Kid"; and Dan Bonar, his brother, talked so much about all the scutching of flax he had done in his young days when he worked for farmers in Northern Ireland, he became better known amongst the men on the job as "Dan the Scutcher". There was another Bonar there, "the Black Bonar", who had been a well known tunnel worker and long distance man in his day, but now like old Cafferkey with Lawrence he was gone past it and had to settle for something easier. Willie Gillanders was a quiet man who did not have much to say. From his unassuming manner one would never think that he had been decorated for bravery in the war. But he made no secret of it that he no longer believed in war. The man had seen so much of it, it made a pacifist out of him. And he had little to show now for his wartime bravery, working by day digging muck and sleeping by night in a model lodging house beside Glasgow Green

Those and others like them made up the personnel of the navvying gangs—the men who dug the founds and the trenches and laid the concrete. With the various squads of tradesmen on the site we did not mix, and even their labourers kept apart from us. For all we had to do with them they might almost have not been there at all. We knew the names of some of them but not all of them. Sometimes one or two of the young apprentices might breach the unwritten rules of etiquette and come in to sit and have the crack in the navvy hut on a wet day but soon they learned that this was not the way of their peers and they conformed.

One tradesman everybody knew was an old bricklayer named Jock Shearer. A man close to retiring age, he spoke in a broad Scots dialect; "the Doric" old Brennan called it. Shearer had at one time been a foreman with the firm but he had been demoted—reduced to working the tools. It was said that he had been a most difficult man to work under and that men could not stick with him. He still did pretty much as he liked, and that included working out in the rain when the rest of us were in the huts. Then he would come into the canteen at tea-time, soaking wet, and muttering about: "the useless kind o' men that is goin' nowadays".

At Stewart's labourers were only allowed half an hours pay for every hour we were rained off. There was only a thirty-two-hour guarantee, and we had no union to back us up like the tradesmen had. They were in the union and so they got their time paid no matter how the weather was. Most of us preferred to sit in the hut on a wet day rather than to stay out working in the rain, for as John the Pole said:

"better be paid half an hour for dry beside the fire than an hour for wet in the rain".

The Scots lads, ever daft about football, let us down one wet day. About a dozen of them were outside, kicking an old ball around, and us all rained off, tradesmen, labourers, the lot. Duncan Glen insisted, and rightly too, that if the day was good enough for playing football it was good enough for working, so he sent everybody out; it was all he could do after how the silly fools had carried on. Stewart came on the scene shortly after, and a good thing we were working, for with all his fairness, and he was fair, old Bob was a strict man, and if he had found some of the men inside, sheltering from the rain, and others outside playing ball, he would have kicked up bloodly hell.

CHAPTER SIXTEEN

Glasgow Life

FROM THE DAY I CAME TO Scotland, on every job I ever worked on, I saw a psuedo-religious conflict go on between the supporters of Celtic and Ranger soccer clubs. I have watched it cause no end of needless animosity amongst working men. For the past hundred years or more the people of Glasgow in particular and Scotland in general have been divided into two opposing soccer camps—Catholics for Celtic and Protestants for Rangers. At first I found it hard to know what to make of it. We never knew anything like that in Mayo—football rivalry revolving around religion. But as John McGinlay, a Donegal man, said: "Glasgow is not Mayo." Religion wasn't really the cause of the conflict, and for many it wasn't football either. It was little more than an excuse for sectarianism, and an excuse to indulge in hooliganism. It was something to identify with, something to shout about and to fight about; the "us" and the "them" mentality. It was the "Papes" and the "Prods" at work, the "Dans" and the "Billys". Many of the most ardent followers of either Celtic or Rangers never went near a chapel or a church, and just as well they did not. They would not have been much of an asset to their churches, and I don't think they were much of an asset to the teams they followed.

Glasgow Celtic Football Club was founded as an Irish Catholic team in the latter part of the nineteenth century for the purpose of raising funds for poor Irish emigrants and their families, and it has retained the support of the Irish Catholic element in Scotland generally ever since, even though it has long ceased being Irish and insists that it is a wholly Scottish club, which in truth it is. In fact they go to great pains to downplay their Irishness and to emphasise their Scottishness.

Rangers, the boys in blue, are the other side of the sectarian coin. They constitute the Protestant-Orange support. Until very recently, Rangers would never sign a Catholic to play for them. Celtic, on the other hand, were quite willing to play Protestants in their team. Many

Protestants have played for them and have been prominent with them over the years; men like the great Jock Stein, whose name will ever be associated with the club, first as a player and later as a manager. I cannot truly say I have ever met a Catholic who was a Rangers supporter, and if I did I should think I would look at him twice, to make sure what colour his nose was. Rangers supporters are supposed to have blue noses, and the more extreme Orange they are the bluer the nose. I have, however, known many Protestants who were Celtic supporters.

Those were the days of the legendary Charlie Tully, the famous Celtic player, and his name was on everybody's lips. I went along to Parkhead a few times to see Tully play. What Irishman in Scotland at the time did not? And I confess I never thought him to be the almighty footballer he was made out to be. He was smart, very smart, that I admit, but I have seen better players.

Charlie had a pub for a while, the "Moy Bar" in Cumberland Street at the corner of Florence Street. At least it was reputed to have been his, but I don't think it really belonged to him. I think he was put in there for the publicity, to draw the crowds. And he did that. The Celtic element came in droves from far and near to drink in "Charlie Tully's pub"; so crowded was the place you could hardly get into it. Charlie himself would be there, standing inside the door (I never saw him behind the bar)—a pleasant soft-faced young man, wearing his Donegal tweed suit and dickie bow tie. And they worshipped the ground he stood on. Old fellows of over eighty came there specially and suffered the crush so that they could see the great man and shake his hand. He was a football legend; he was an Irishman, and he could make the Rangers players look silly, so he was a hero in their eyes and they loved him. Some unlikely tales have been told over the years about Tully's remarkable prowess on the field of play. There was one story which went something as follows.

Celtic were playing against Hibernian at Easter Road, Edinburgh. The team bus broke down on the way, with the result none of the Celtic players got there on time, except Charlie who had travelled by car. At kick-off time he took to the field, alone, against the whole Hibs side. At half-time, when the other ten Celtic players arrived, Celtic was winning 1 – 0, Tully having scored a goal. The whole Celtic team played in the second half and at the end the final score was the same as at half-time: Celtic 1 – Hibs 0. Don't believe it. There is not a word of truth in it. It never happened.

In July 1971 I was saddened to hear of Charlie Tully's death in his native Belfast, at the age of forty-seven. He was a man who gave much pleasure to many people.

There was one big red-headed Donegal lassie in the south side in those days—a bus conductress—and she was Celtic obsessed if anyone ever was. She was forever knitting sweaters for the team, and she had the Celtic colours up all over the house, and all over herself too. I remember one time she was reported in the newspapers as saying she never wanted to have a boyfriend. "The eleven boys in green and while are good enough for me", she said. As far as I know she never did get a man of her own, not that she cared; as long as she had Celtic she had all she wanted.

One man, who was regarded as practically an uncanonised saint in Celtic circles, was goalkeeper Johnny Thomson, who was accidentally killed in a game against Rangers at Ibrox. A picture of him in his polo neck jersey could be seen in many of a Glasgow-Irish home, hanging on the wall in the place of honour, often next to the Pope. In one house I saw him between the Pope and Robert Emmett. Thomson, like Emmett, was a Protestant. In tribute to him I include here a balled which over the years has passed his name on to generations to whom 1931, the year he died, must seem like ancient history.

The Ballad of Johnny Thomson

I took a trip to Parkhead, to the dear old Paradise,
As the teams made their appearance, the tears fell from my
    eyes.
A familiar face was missing from the green and white
    brigade,
It was the face of Johnny Thomson, for his last game he had
    played.

There was a lad named Johnny Thomson, from the west of
    Fife he came,
To play for Glasgow Celtic and win himself a name.
It was the fifth day of September against Rangers club did
    play,
Celtic won the honours, but what a price to pay.

145

The game was not long started when the Rangers got the
    ball,
They gave it to Sam English, he went straight for Celtic's
    goal.
He beat Cook and then McGonagle, but with Thomson still
    to beat,
It was then our darling hero died at the centre's feet.

The fans they all fell silent, they had come from near and far,
To see young Johnny Thomson for he was their guiding star.
Play up, you Glasgow Celtic, and keep up the old brigade,
No more you see John Thomson for his last game he has
    played.
Farewell to you, John Thomson, for the best of friends must
    part,
No more we will stand and cheer you from the slopes of
    Celtic Park.

It can be a highly charged atmosphere in certain Glasgow pubs on a
Saturday night and intoxicating in more ways than one when the boys
in green and white have done well that day. And when that and other
Celtic songs are sung, it's hard to keep from getting carried away by
it all.

It was at the Fair in July that I left the Spittal and the employment of
Bob Stewart. I had been there for almost a year and that made me a
sticker compared to some. To men of my generation a year was then
a long time to have been on any one job, so I saw myself as a man
with something of a record in that respect. Many of the fellows I
knew socially were the same as me in that they hardly ever left the
greater Glasgow area. But they never stayed long in the same job;
they moved about from site to site, and from contractor to contractor,
working maybe a fortnight in one place, six weeks in another, a few
months perhaps in a third, according as they took the notion. As Denis
Carey said: "A man gets fed up looking at the same bit of muck the
whole time."

They were looked down upon by the "long distance kiddies"—the
men who roved the country chasing the big money. The more a man
moved about and the rougher his lifestyle the more he was looked up
to in navvy circles. "See that man", as some tough-looking character

of a roving Irishman would be pointed out in the pub, "he has been in every town in Scotland, thinks nothing of sleeping out under the bush." They took an inverted pride in having tramped the length and breadth of the land and they were admired for it.

I did not stay idle throughout the holiday week that year. I went out and got started with the Scottish Special Housing Association on the building of Toryglen, one of the few building projects that continued working during the holiday period. Tommy Brown was the ganger. Tommy was a North of Ireland man, a young man with a small moustache like the one Clark Gable had. He kicked with the wrong foot, that is to say he was not one of ours—he was an Orangeman. But he was all right to work under; for the few weeks I was there I found no loss of him; I found him to be as good and better than many of my own religion.

I had been at a friend's wedding earlier that summer. The reception was in the Central Hall in Jamaica Street, and it ended in a fracas. I am not sure how the fighting started; I think it had something to do with the dividing of the drink. It was said that one of the brides's uncles complained about the unfairness of the way in which some Irish poteen, that had been smuggled over specially for the occasion, was being distributed—certain well-wishers being called aside and given a drink of it. Others who thought themselves equally entitled to a share got none. Anyhow, it came to blows and, as I said, I am not sure how it started, but I know how it finished. It ended in a free-for-all with people hitting each other all over the place, even the women wading in, walloping away with their handbags. It was like Finnigan's wake in the song.

As far as I remember, only two people in the hall took no part in the fighting that night, and they were a big Galway man named Mick Caulfield and myself. We stood on two chairs watching the fun and I think those were about the only two chairs in the hall that escaped injury, the others were used as weapons. And then the police arrived and we were all ejected. Mick and I walked across Jamaica Bridge and back to our digs while scuffling continued outside the hall and several were arrested. The papers found out and put on a big splash about it next day under the heading: "Fighting breaks out at Irish Wedding. Hall wrecked."

I left Toryglen and started with Balfour and Beattie in Clydebank and I wintered it there. For most of the time I was banksman to the digger, an easy job, and that was why I stuck it so long: the pay wasn't that good. I left at the end of January after an altercation with a ganger named Meehan, who jarred me for going to the toilet twice the one day. I told him where to stick his job and I jacked once again.

By this time I was staying in McFadden's in Cleland Street, where I was one of about a dozen lodgers. I had been out of Hannigan's for some time and had been in a house in Lawmoor Street, a good place for anybody on a slimming diet, which I was not, and therefore I decided to look for somewhere else. The next place I tried, a house called Connolly's, was full up, and she directed me to McFadden's.

McFadden's was a west Donegal Gaelic-speaking household. It was a house where a fellow was all right as long as he was able to take fun, kept reasonably sober and tidy, and attended to his religious duties. These things were expected from him and without them he would not be long there. It was a house where a stranger could feel at home, with an Irish welcome and an Irish hospitality. It was clean and well kept, the food and the crack was good, and I have many happy memories of the time I spent there. It was also a full house.

Besides two full rooms of lodgers a third room was occupied by the landlady's two young sisters, Mary and Annie, and by another girl Nellie McCafferty who got married while I was there. I thought Annie, the youngest of the two sisters (she was about seventeen), was one of the most attractive girls I had ever seen. Mary was a few years older and very religious minded—Legion of Mary stuff and all that. "Holy Mary" we used to call her. She was not so holy sounding when she got annoyed and she got many things to be annoyed about. Often when we came in at night after been at the pictures or somewhere, we used to go into the girls' room, and there would be Mary, down on her knees beside the bed, saying her novenas. And we would start tormenting her, and it was then the strange words could get mixed up with the prayers.

The tormenting was not all one-sided. Mary was well able to do a bit herself, both her and Annie, and Nellie too. Other girls, friends from home, came visiting nearly every night, the same as in Ireland, and between the lot of them they done plenty tormenting on us.

They used to interfere with the bedclothes so that we got tangled up in the sheets when we went to bed. One night, nettles, wherever they found them, were put into our beds. A favourite trick of theirs was to sew the leg of a man's trousers across at the bottom so that he couldn't get them on in the morning when he got up in a hurry rushing to get to his work. But if your trousers needed sewing they would not

148

sew them for you. They would watch not to do that. The landlady herself never discouraged those harmless pranks which went on, indeed she was not above taking part in them. Joe, her husband, was a quiet civil man. I never saw him vexed, nor would I have liked to, and I never saw him drunk. He was always the same—a good family man who worked hard for five and a half days every week, and always on Saturday afternoons during the football season he went to see the game; that was his relaxation, the weekly football match.

Many years later, after I had lost touch with the family, I saw Joe McFadden's picture in the paper one morning. The article below it told of how he had a narrow escape from death, due to a gas leakage in a heading (underground boring) where he was working. He was saved by the bravery of his mates who went back in to rescue him. I was glad he was all right. The McFadden's were nice people; they had a jolly crowd of lodgers, male and female, and I was happy there.

In those days the Irish anti-partition League was going full swing. It was very active in Scotland and had strong support, not only amongst the native-born Irish, but more so amongst people of second and third generation Irish descent. The league ran candidates in one general election and although none of them polled heavily they did not do too badly for a fringe group. They hurt the Labour candidates most; Conservative supporters would not have anything to do with them, and so they served to split the Labour vote. It had long been a tradition for the Irish in Scotland to vote Labour.

The league never seemed to tire of holding public meetings in halls, and they were able to draw sizeable crowds to their meetings. They were also well able to produce VIP guest speakers, including several British and Irish Members of Parliament. Another thing they went in for in a big way was gathering money for their cause. It used to be jokingly said that they intended to buy the six counties from Britain; others said they were collecting it for themselves. I don't know. After a while they faded away not having been seen to have achieved anything much, except perhaps the publicity. It would take more than a storm of hot air to blow away the border.

One thing I noticed in Scotland was that more marriages took place and on the whole people married younger than in Ireland. Also whenever a relationship developed between a young couple there was more of a chance of it leading to something serious—an engagement,

149

and in due course, a marriage. In Ireland a couple might keep company for years seemingly without ever thinking of marrying, or if they thought of it that was all they done about it. Some eventually did marry, when they were old enough to have their families reared. Others never got round to it. And sometimes an old cod of a man, long past his best, and after having wasted the best years of a girl's life, went off and married someone else, for the sake of getting a younger woman, or one with a bit of land, or a dowry of a few head of cattle. I knew several couples who went together for six or seven years and never married and I knew of one long drawn-out courtship of over twenty years duration which came to nothing in the end.

In rural Ireland courtship had a guilt complex attached to it. If you were going along the road at night and met a couple who were romantically involved, more often than not, they would try to conceal their identity. They would even leave the road and go in behind a ditch or a turf stack to avoid meeting a neighbour, and then come out on to the road again once the coast was clear, whatever it was they were afraid of. By acting in that way they were making it look as if they were up to no good when in fact they were doing nothing wrong and had nothing whatsoever to be ashamed of. I think the priests with their unreasonable attitude towards "company-keeping" were to a large extent responsible for this strange behaviour, as were the older people with their prying and their scandal-mongering. From the way some of them talked you would think they never done the likes themselves.

In Scotland when a pair who were "winching" walked out together they did so openly and made no secret of their relationship. Meet them in the street and they would not try to hide or run away. They would introduce the boyfriend or the girlfriend as the case might be. They visited each others' homes and got to know each others' people. Now wasn't that better than the way in Ireland—hiding behind the ditches sooner than be seen together. Whoever caused people who had nothing to hide to act in such a secretive and guilt-ridden manner, I would say they have a lot to answer for.

Homosexuality was a condition that I never knew existed until I came to Scotland, though by the laws of average we must have had homosexuals in the district where I grew up. If any of the lads around our place at home were like that, then I must say they kept it well to themselves. Sex education was a thing we never got; at home, in the school, nor anywhere, except the wrong kind, from dirty jokers who

150

wished to spread their knowledge of such matters. Nor did we know of other perversions such as child sex abuse which we hear so much about nowadays.

All that is past and gone now and has been succeeded by another style of things as different to the old style as chalk and cheese. They know it all now. All the censorship did not keep it away from them, only made them less prepared for it when it came. The permissive age hit Ireland all of a sudden and with a hard impact. A way of life has emerged there now that the people of my grandfather's day would hardly recognise. The old values have gone by the board. The sanctity of marriage seems to be a thing of the past. The devil has been made redundant or so it seems, and the priest no longer worries about the company-keepers or vice versa. No longer is there any respect for the aged or for the infirm, nor for other people's property, nor for anything nor anybody for that matter. Crime is commonplace all over the country as is drug taking amongst the young. Alcoholism has tainted every section of the community, young and old, rich and poor, clergy and laity alike. Changed days!

CHAPTER SEVENTEEN

Time to Jack

AFTER LEAVING BALFOUR and Beattie I went back again to work in Toryglen. I do not think the management was aware that I had been there before or if they were they gave no indication of it. It was a place where so many men came and went that it was hard to remember them all. I remember well the day I started there the second time. Pat Houston from Donegal was out on the bus with me. He had come up from England to marry his childhood sweetheart who was now a bus conductress with Glasgow Corporation and we both went out and got put to work with the Scottish Special Housing Association.

The travelling ganger there now was a man named Tommy Boyce, but he soon left and was replaced by Paddy McLaughlinn. For most of my second term there my ganger was Paddy Ferry. Ferry was a friend and old workmate of McLaughlinn. He was no ganger the first time I was there, only a pipelayer, and I will say this for him, he was a good pipelayer. He was a first class man at his job and he loved to admire his own handiwork. "There is nothing nicer than a neatly laid line of pipes", he would say as he looked along the drain with his head to one side and him chewing tobacco. Everyone, I suppose, is entitled to their opinion, but to my mind there are many nicer things than sewer pipes, no matter how well they are laid down. "No need to be half so fussy", said Boyce who did not like him. Luckily for Ferry, Boyce was moved, and the new man McLaughinn lost no time in promoting his old crony to full gangership.

Ferry the ganger would grumble and complain about the least thing. He was a hard man to put up with and one by one the old hands of the squad fell out with him or got fed up with his narking and went away. That was about all they could do; there was no use taking the matter up with McLaughlinn and they knew it. So they jacked up. The men who came to fill their places never knew Ferry as anything but a ganger and that was how he wanted it. He was glad to be rid of the old hands.

We left Toryglen in late Spring, got moved to another site adjacent to the Maryhill crematorium. Funerals arrived daily, sometimes several a day, at the incinerating plant across the road. About fifteen or twenty minutes after a funeral went in smoke would be seen ascending from the lum. Sometimes the smoke would be black and thick looking and then we thought they were burning a fat, well-nourished corpse in there. Paddy McColum said that if the smoke went straight up it was a sure sign the soul had gone to heaven. Mick Conroy said it was a surer sign of a calm day.

One fine day in summer I bade farewell to the Scottish Special Housing Association for ever. Ferry remained in their employment for the rest of his working life. As he said when I met him again several years later, where else would he have got it so easy, and he was right; nothing to do only stand over other men all day and make them do the work. In his old age he used to complain bitterly, I was told, about how shabbily the firm treated him in the end: paid him off the day he was sixty-five, although he would have liked to work on for a few more years, and never gave him a presentation or anything else, "after all the good work I done for them". Perhaps he got as good as he deserved. Time there was when he did not have much mercy, when he was the cause of men leaving their jobs, and he did not care three hoots; but the day came when he himself was told to go and then he did not like it. It is a long road that has not an end or a turn somewhere and time is a great leveller.

Over the next few years I worked for a number of building and civil engineering contractors. I changed jobs whenever the mood came on me. In one place, at the building of a new school, I stayed for a whole eight months. That was the longest; in most cases it was a matter of spending six weeks or a couple of months on a site, and then get fed up and go somewhere else. They were all pretty much alike; better money could be earned on some than on others—when they were in a hurry to get the job completed within a certain time, but seldom did that last for long. If I was on a job and the overtime was cut down I would jack and go off to look for another site with good overtime on it. Sometimes I left on my own, sometimes in the company of others. Casey, Heraghty, Lynch and myself worked together on several building sites in and around Glasgow in those years.

I was never paid off or sacked from any job and that is a thing every man cannot say. Unfair dismissals were thick and plenty in those days and there was nothing the poor labourer could do. It was different with the tradesmen; they had their unions to their back; they were organised, the labourers were not. The one time I was dismissed I would not call it a dismissal.

In Kincardine nobody liked working in the cement shed, and that was no wonder because it was a rotten job, handling bags of cement the whole time, all day, every day of the week, unloading it from the lorries as they came in, stacking it up in piles as high as the roof, and then reloading it again, on to tractors to be taken around to the concreting squads and to the batching plant. This constant handling of cement burned the hands, and the cement dust got into the eyes and the ears, and up the nostrils, and down the throat and into the lungs. It matted the hair. (One man who worked at the batching plant—Owen Ferry—kept his scalp shaved Yul Brynner fashion.) And that only mentions a few of the unpleasant and unhealthy aspects of working full-time with cement. It was known to cause skin infections such as dermatitis, and it was said that any man who worked for any length of time constantly handling cement and breathing in its dust never lived for any more than a few years afterwards. I knew a few men who worked in cement sheds and batching plants and they died young, whether the cement caused their deaths or not, I do not know, but I don't think it helped them. Nowadays, men would not be asked to do that kind of work without proper equipment and protection. We were not asked to do it, we were ordered to, and it was either obey or go. One foreman I knew, himself an Irishman, bad cess to him, said, "If they don't do it, others will. They are coming off the boat every morning."

I refused to work in the cement shed not only because I wanted to live for more that just another few years, but also because when I had worked in it for a few days in place of a man who was off sick, it irritated my bad eye. When the sick man left I was put on to it again. I refused to do it. I did not say it was because of my eye as I did not want to admit I had a bad eye. I said I was refusing because the last time I was there I was not paid the two pence per hour extra which was my rightful entitlement for working on that particular job. That too was true but it was not my main reason for refusing. The travelling ganger told me I was being paid a labourer's wage—three shillings an hour—and that was good enough for me, and as much as I was worth, and if I did not like it I could go down the road. So I went down the road and had no regrets. I started on a better job the following morning. I would have regretted it had I given in to that old mini-tyrant, and that was all he was. I had not noticed on my cards when I got them that the word "dismissed" was written on them. The foreman on the new job noticed it at once but he did not fault me for it when I explained the situation to him. He was a decent man, not like some of my own countrymen.

The Irish navvy ganger would not be long thinking about telling a man to go down the road, and without much regards for the rights or the wrongs of the matter. Standing over the workers, with his thumbs in his waistcoat pocket, his crooked pipe in his mouth, and the threepence an hour extra in his pay packet, he was the cock of the walk, he was like the rooster on the top of the dunghill. And he showed no mercy to the fowl scraping about below him.

Now in their declining years, those gangers, any of them who still survive, and that is not many, if you mention to them about how hard they were on the workers, they say they were only doing what they were told. Away from their work they were a sanctimonious old lot: a good many of them were great chapel goers and church workers, going around with the plate at Mass on Sundays, taking up the collection for the priest, and walking in processions—that sort of thing. They liked to project themselves as visible and upright pillars of the parish. They made an open show of their christianity but at the same time they intensified the hardships of those who worked under them. Not only that, they cheated them whenever they could. Out at their work they were slave drivers and rogues. Regardless of how good any man was as a worker, if the ganger did not like him he gave him a hard time of it. Often if there was bonus on the job they contrived to fiddle it, to misappropriate it, so that they and their pals got the lion's share. Now I am not saying they were all like that, but a good portion of them were. The straight decent man was to be found amongst them, but he was in the minority and taking them in general a Scottish ganger was a better man to work under than an Irish one.

A navvy ganger, no mater how important he thought he was or tried to make himself out to be, was in reality not much more that a glorified labourer. Like the rest of us he could be sacked at a moment's notice. The main attribute of a typical ganger man was often not so much his knowledge as his ignorance. A man with a dominant personality coupled with servility towards his bosses was ready-made for the job, toadying up to those who were over him, and bullying those who were under him. And that is how the majority of them were, and if there are still people around who don't like what I say, too bad. It happens to be true.

Funny stories went the rounds about some of them. There was the one about a ganger-cum-Sunday chapel pass-keeper who was accosted by the prostitute one night up at Blythswood Square. Thirty shillings she wanted from him for her services for a short time up the lane. He offered her a pound but no more. It was not worth thirty shillings he said. She let him go with the parting shot, "you won't get much for your pound." He was up the town again the following week, himself and his wife, to see a show in the Pavilion, and who did they meet face to face in Hope Street but the same woman and she recognised him. She paused and looked his wife up and down in a most scrutinising manner: "I telt ye you wouldn't get much for ye'r pound", she said.

I don't know if somebody was listening or if somebody made it up. It might never have happened and again I suppose it could happen to nearly any man, but after I heard that no matter where I saw that bloke I always thought of it. And he was so upright and religious minded, at least in public. He used to remind me of Rabbie Burns' "Holly Willie".

With no evening Mass in those days, a good true practising Catholic who worked Sundays got up and went to early Mass, usually six o'clock in the morning. It was the same for holidays of obligation and we had more of them then than we have now. It was committing a mortal sin to wilfully miss Mass on a Sunday or on a church holiday and that was the worst calamity that could happen to anyone—to fall into mortal sin. It was hell's fire for anyone so unfortunate as to die in that tragic state. As we were oft and many a time reminded by our spiritual advisers, we had only one life to live, one soul to save. Death would soon come, judgment would follow, and then heaven or hell for all eternity. And anyone who died in mortal sin was lost for ever. Was it any wonder that we got up and went to six o'clock Mass every Sunday we were working.

But what pleased the church did not always please the landlady. "Nobody in this house is going to get up making breakfasts for you on Sunday mornings early", I was told in one digs I stayed in. I did not ask her to make breakfasts. I got up and went out without my

156

breakfast, and I still felt I had a good bargain: I saved myself from the risk of going to hell and I got two days' pay for one day's work, either of which was well worth going without breakfast for.

One man I knew, a chargehand on the railway, whose job made it necessary for him to work Sundays, told me the priest advised him that if he could not attend Mass he should consider changing his job. And he had been on the railway nearly all his working life, a man with a home and a wife and young children to support. I don't know what he did as regards attending Mass, but he did not change his job; he remained on the railway until he retired. The man was doing his best; he was earning an honest living in the only way he knew how, and he had to work seven days a week. To my mind he does not deserve to go to hell when he dies. And regarding holidays of obligation, I don't think it a bit fair that people will be burning and roasting below in hell for all eternity because they wilfully missed Mass, say on the nineteenth of March or on the eighth of December, twenty or thirty years ago, while we can do it now and it's no sin at all.

The parish priest in St Luke's in the south side was Fr Martin, a stocky and dogmatic County Sligo man. Amongst his parishioners he was known as a contrary man, though I doubt if many of them would dare tell him that up to his face. He could not stand people coughing in the chapel when he was giving out the Sunday sermon, and a fiery, long-winded sermon he could make, the same man. I recall one Sunday and the coughing was bad. There was a cold going around at the time and a cough with it, but a great many people who had it went to Mass just the same; they would not stay away for fear of damnation. As Fr Martin laboured on with his sermon he became more and more irritated by the coughing which went on at the same time. The longer he spoke the more they coughed until at last he could take no more. Pulling out his big watch he announced that he was giving the congregation three minutes coughing time; anyone with coughing to do was to do it now or hold their peace until he had finished. But did they take advantage of the break to cough enough? Not a bit of it; instead of the coughing increasing it slackened off. Then when the three minutes were up the priest started talking again. And guess what! The coughing broke out again, worse than ever. It would not have been done on purpose; it would have been a nervous reaction I suppose, but whatever it was it exasperated the priest so much he gave it up for a bad job. He stomped off the pulpit and we never heard the end of the sermon.

Many a good scolding from the pulpit Fr Martin gave to Joe Stalin, the Russian dictator, the number one enemy of the Catholic church at that time. "The day is fast approaching", he would thunder, hitting the pulpit with his fist, "when his rotten carcass will be the food of worms. The years are closing around him and very soon he will pass into the great beyond. His day of reckoning is coming and he will not go by it." As if the same did not apply to all of us as well as to Stalin, whose day is now long gone. It comes to everybody sooner or later.

The one thing Fr Martin would never do was to officiate at a mixed marriage—the marriage of a Catholic to a non-Catholic. Where he was concerned that was out—he just would not do it. Anybody wanting to make a mixed marriage had to go to some other clergyman. I wonder what would he say now when about half of them shack up together without bothering to get married and about one marriage in every three breaks up. Taking everything into consideration I would say, in all fairness to him, he was a good man but very shirty. He was acting in the way he thought best for the welfare of his flock and according to the lights of the times. Things have changed since then.

CHAPTER EIGHTEEN

An Unexpected Journey

IN 1952 I WAS LODGING in O'Kane's in Thistle Street, Mrs McFadden having got rid of her lodgers when it suited her purpose. She needed more house room for her increasing family and we were told to go, all but the two sisters; they were allowed to stay in their rooms. Lodgers had no fixity of tenure; it was often a matter of here today and away tomorrow, so we took it in our stride; we packed up and left before the happy event—the new addition came along. Afterwards I heard that she let one of the rooms to a newly married couple (Neillie and her man) and that was easier any day and a lot less work than looking after lodgers.

O'Kane's flat was at the top of a dark stair in a dark close but it was a very good house to stay in, as good a digs, I believe, taking all in, as there was in the south side. Paddy Moy and myself had a room to ourselves and that was a luxury compared to some places where they slept six, and eight, and even ten men to a room.

My local on Saturday nights was the Ritz Bar at the corner of Rutherglen Road and Florence Street, only a stone's throw away from the lodgings. It was owned by two Sligo brothers, Pat and Andy Connor. The clientele were mostly Irishmen and it was interesting to listen to them, talking about all the places where they had worked and so forth. They talked a lot about their work and the more they drank the more they talked. "Don't go over near that end of the bar, they are blasting out headings over there", said Ballysodare man John Conlon. And when they were not blasting out headings they were boring tunnels and if it wasn't that it was something else.

A scruffy old fellow named Ned Scanlan would be lurking on the outer edges of the groups of men engrossed in discussing work, in order to drink any spare beer left lying around. He was a fly old boy who would not be long finishing off an unguarded pint if he got half a chance, so if you needed to go to the toilet it was worth asking your mate to keep an eye on your drink while you were away, or you might come back to find your glass empty and old Ned looking like the cat that got at the cream.

Landlady Sally O'Kane did not reckon much of public houses. "Going down to the dirty old pub ye's are, filling up ye'er bellies with beer", she used to say. Sally claimed that she had never been inside a public house in her life. Well, if that was the way that suited her, good luck to her, it did not suite everybody. There are far worse things a man can do than drink a couple of pints on a Saturday night after working hard all week.

One foggy Friday evening in November on coming in from work I found a letter from home awaiting me. It was from my mother telling me she had to go to Dr Stevens' Hospital in Dublin for to undergo an operation. She was writing in the hope I would go over and visit her; she would like to see me, and if I could be there to meet her when she arrived that would be better still as she did not know Dublin. She was going on Monday, on the bus, she said, and now it was Friday evening. I wanted to go to meet her, but money was the problem—I did not have enough. The week previous I had sent my father a few pounds to put into the Belmullet bank for me; I never kept much money about me in Scotland. I had enough to take me to Dublin but not enough to keep me there for a few days and to bring me back again. It was Mrs O'Kane who gave me the money—fifteen pounds —and she proved a good friend when I needed one, and that is when you find out who your friends are—when you need them. Fifteen pounds was as good then as two hundred is now, easily. It was not every landlady would do it.

I sailed from the Clyde on Saturday night on the Belfast boat so as to meet my mother on Monday. There was no other way I could do it as there were no direct sailings between Glasgow and Dublin at weekends. It was foggy on the Clyde that night and it was cold. I remember standing on the deck, and not a sinner there only myself, watching the seagulls circling and screaming as they accompanied the boat, and often when I threw bits of bread to them they were able to catch them before they hit the water. The gulls always came with us for part of the way until we were met by Irish gulls from the other side.

We were in Belfast very early in the morning. I got the train to Dublin, breakfasted in the Erin Restaurant in Talbot Street, and then it being Sunday, I went to Mass in the Pro-Cathedral around the corner.

That night I went to the pictures in the Hippodrome along the road from the bed and breakfast place where I had booked in. While standing in the queue waiting to get in I fell into conversation with three people, a middle-aged woman and her son and daughter who were in their late teens or early twenties: the daughter was the oldest of the two. When finally we were let in the usher mistook us to be the one company and gave us seats beside each other, and afterwards at the interval we shared ice-cream and sweets. The three of them were alike, short and broad and Dublin spoken. They lived in Marlborough Street and kept a fruit stall in the open air market off O'Connell Street, they told me. And they went to the pictures nearly every night, they said. They were friendly sociable people, kindly to a stranger, but not the kind of people I would care to come on the wrong side of; I would say they would be able to hold their own anywhere. I visited that picture house twice again in the coming week and they were there each time and again we sat together. On the night before I left Dublin, after the programme ended, we all had tea in the cafe across the road. I took down their address and promised the daughter I would write to her, and she promised that if I wrote she would write back. And then when she thought her mother wasn't looking she pressed her small hand over mine. That was the nearest I got to her. I never got round to writing to her: had I done so who knows what might have come out of it. I might be selling apples and oranges from a stall in Moore Street today.

On Monday evening I went down to the Liffeyside—to Aston Quay, to meet the Ballina bus. My mother was one of the last to get off. Two men from Surgeview, Blacksod, a young man named Patrick Walsh, and his uncle, a man of about fifty, had been with her the whole way from Belmullet, and she said, "they were nice company, two grand fellows". It was the same Patrick Walsh, I believe, who some years ago was accidentally drowned when his curragh capsized within yards of the shore. May God rest his soul.

That was the last time I saw buses from the west coming into Aston Quay. I was aware there would soon be a change as I had overheard a man talking in the dining-room of the bed and breakfast place, telling some Americans about the new bus depot they were building at Store Street. It was going to be the biggest in Europe, he said. That man knew how to talk in their own language to those boastful Americans who thought they had everything bigger and better than anybody else.

My mother was tired after her whole day's travelling, but in good spirits nonetheless; she was better than I had expected her to be. After something to eat in the Erin we went to the hospital by bus. She settled in nicely. The staff could not have been kinder or more helpful, and she did not have to wait long for the operation; she had it the very next morning. When I went in to see her that evening (Tuesday) she looked weak and did not have much to say. That was to be expected, the ward sister explained, as she was only a few hours out of the anaesthetic and the operation had been a serious one—the removal of a stomach tumour. On Wednesday I saw a marked improvement in her condition and she was better still on Thursday. I left Dublin on Friday afternoon and returned to Glasgow by the same route as I had come.

During my few days in Ireland's capital I managed to visit some of the places that I had often heard and read about but never seen. I was in Trinity College, in the National Library, in the Museum, and in the public gallery of the Dáil in Leinster House. I climbed the weary long stairs to the top of Nelson's Pillar, afterwards blown up by the IRA, and enjoyed a magnificent view of Dublin and its surroundings from there.

The Dáil I found to be a dull, boring place about three-quarters empty. Of the several members who spoke on the evening I was there, the only one I thought worth listening to was Michael Donnellan, a loud and gruff-spoken man, swarty in appearance, and with a strong western brogue: he fairly livened up the place while he spoke. Donnellan had in his young days been a famous Gaelic footballer. Well known footballers, like retired paramilitary gunmen, have always had a way of getting themselves elected into the Dáil. Popular figures in the people's imagination, they have about them an aura of glamour which makes them great vote-catchers at elections even if some of them are not much good as politicians. Donnellan was good though.

On Friday I was on the Belfast boat again going back to Glasgow, and without many fellow passengers, only two or three others besides myself travelled steerage. I do not know how many were in the first class department, but we had a fair number of four-legged passengers —the cattle down in the hold. They were driven off at Whiteinch pier amid the usual loud din and hammering with sticks. The rest of us carried on up to the Broomielaw.

I thought Glasgow looked black and grimy compared to Dublin,

162

which was a very clean city at that time. But it is not like that any more. I would say Glasgow is by far the cleaner city of the two now, and I would say as well that it is the safer city of the two to go about in, notwithstanding the bad name that has been given to Glasgow over the years.

My mother spent four weeks in hospital and she made a good recovery. My intention was to go over again and take her home, but she wrote to say there was no need and not to put the expense on myself as an ambulance travelled to Castlebar every week and she would go down on it and my father would come to Castlebar to meet her. But as things turned out she did not go on the ambulance, for who walked into the ward one day but Belmullet hackney driver Sonny Henaghan. He had taken a patient to the hospital in his car and knowing my mother was there he went in to see her. It ended up with her getting discharged a day early and going home with Sonny. He took her home to her own door for the same money as she had paid on the bus coming up, and that was better than the ambulance which had the reputation of being very bumpy and hard on people after operations.

That winter passed, dark and dreary and cold like every winter. I was working in Duntocher with a firm called Atholl and although I was staying in Glasgow I never saw the daylight in it for three or four months—working seven days a week, going to work in the dark mornings, up before six o'clock and already working before the break of dawn, and dark again before we finished at night. The daylight is not with us as long in Scotland in wintertime as it is in Ireland because Scotland is much further north. My routine away from work varied but little with the seasons except that I hardly ever went to the park; apart from that it was nearly the same all year around—the pictures at night a few times every week, the beer at the weekend and the Irish dancing on Sunday nights.

As no pubs opened on Sundays some thirsty men went out regularly for a sabbath drink to hotels in the country. I never did that, thought sometimes I visited the Railway Hotel in Buchanan Street on Sunday nights for an hour or two. All one needed to do to get in was to sign the book, giving an address outside of Glasgow, and then you could go in and drink as much as you liked. For me the place had an added attraction in the person of the attractive Donegal girl who served the bar. That romance fell through after a while but we remained good friends for many years. She used to visit my wife and

I in our first house in Batson Street, and then she left Scotland to marry a lucky fellow and settle at home. Like many more of my old time friends, male and female, I have not heard trace of her now for many years.

CHAPTER NINETEEN

Cons and a Coronation

THE DAYS OF THE "SPIVS", the shady wartime and post wartime conmen who specialised in black market dealings and other twilight commercial activities in a smallish, but big enough way to earn them a living in the lean years of war-related shortages, came to an end in the early fifties. But still plenty of shadowy denizens kept floating around ready to cash in on the naive and the unwary. In those days when bookmakers agents took bets at street corners at least one crooked duo in the south side, the "false bookie" and his accomplice —one tall and distinguished-looking, the other dumpy and short— had a good run and swindled many a poor devil out of a few pounds before they were caught and put away. They were no bookies at all, only a pair of crooks posing as bookies. I am not rightly sure how they put on their act but it had something to do with "inside information" about sure winners, and they kept changing the location of their operations the whole time. It must have been a plausible act they had as I heard it deceived may a one causing some to part with sizeable sums of money. Young Irish fellows fresh from the country were their main targets. It was said they took one hundred and fifty pounds off one lad who had come down from the north to get married and that he committed suicide— threw himself into the Clyde. I heard afterwards that one of them—the tall one—died in jail, whatever became of the other. He will probably be dead by now too, and not much of a loss.

The false bookies were by no means the only ones out to con the green and the innocent. One man I knew was nicely tricked when he bought a bottle of what he thought was bargain whiskey from a man who accosted him one night outside the Central Station. According to the guy who was selling it, it was one from a case that fell off the back of a lorry. Strange how it did not get broken in the fall! And as it had come so easy he was selling it dog cheap, for about half-price. The fella, thinking he had hit lucky, bought it and took it along to a party he was going to in Govanhill. He got a bad let down when he opened it in front of all the company and found it contained not whiskey but weak tea. He went up the town again the following night, vowing vengeance, looking for the man who had tricked him. What would he not do to him if he caught him! He did not find the man, but instead he nearly got himself arrested for loitering with intent, or some such alleged offence. The police did not believe his story, or at least they said they did not believe it. As soon as they heard him speaking with an Irish accent that was enough: they came down on him like a ton of bricks. He was up to no good, they told him, sculking around the red light district at night, and they made it very clear to him that if they caught him there again he was for the lock up. So he came back down to the south side a sadder and a wiser man.

Another con was the enticing young lady on the look out for the amorous male whose sense of caution was not equal in strength to his sex urge. Having lured him into her apartment by the prospect of pleasures to come, it was usually no problem getting him manoeuvred into a compromising position. And that was the point when the man purporting to be her irate husband and his friends burst in. After being given a good kicking, the intensity of which might or might not depend on how much resistance he offered, the hapless mug was then thrown out bodily into the street after being relieved of his wallet and his watch, and in some cases, minus his trousers. One man to which that particular misfortune befell was picked up by the police as he made his way back to his lodgings without any trousers on. It was on a Friday night he was caught and he nearly died from the cold lying in the cell until Monday morning—it being the month of March. His lumbar regions, I believe, were never the same again after it. He was fined ten pounds for breach of the peace, however they made out that that was what he did.

People were not saints then any more than now but one thing I will say for them, even the worst of them seldom resorted to the brutal muggings and cowardly attacks on the weak and the elderly which are so commonplace now. The street gangs were active and violent. They waged their own little wars amongst themselves, using a varied assortment of weaponry such as razors, chains, hammers, and knives, but in general they did not interfere with people who had no involvement with them. I was not long in Glasgow when I was told, regarding the gangs, "If you don't bother them they won't bother you", and that, I think, at the time was fair enough comment. Not so now.

The Coronation of Queen Elizabeth the Second which took place on the second day of June 1953 was the big event of the year. For weeks beforehand it was the talk everywhere, it and the conquest of Mount Everest, the highest mountain in the world—staged so as to coincide with the Coronation, in order to give Britain a double boost of publicity. And they made sure it was Hilary who was photographed on the topmost tip of the mountain, higher than the Sherpa Tenzing, the man who according to some sources pulled him up the last few steps.

Some of the Scottish people tried to argue that the new Queen should not be called Elizabeth the Second because the first Elizabeth, the "Good Queen Bess" of sixteenth-century fame, had never reigned over Scotland. Be that as it may they were quite happy to have this Elizabeth reign over them. "God save our Queen, our glorious Queen, our gracious Queen, Long to reign o'er us", etc. etc. I was sick listening to them and their dose of rubbish.

The Scottish are a queer lot. By any large they are a brave enough people, and they possess a goodly share of national pride, yet they have meekly accepted English rule from London, pandering to their English overlords for the past three hundred years. They are a hard people to fathom. Their own national poet, Robert Burns, called them a parcel of rogues for having sold their country for English gold. And Burns had a way of putting things in their right perspective. The man who sells his nationhood betrays his native land.

Royalty has always been a useful distraction for taking people's minds away from the important issues, such as the plight of the poor, the sick and the unemployed. I say, the kings and queens of hearts, diamonds, clubs and spades should be enough. Queens are all very well for the bees and the wasps; we humans should be able to manage without them.

Preparations for the big day went on for weeks on end until the whole city resembled a gigantic spider's web of flags and bunting of every hue and colour under the sun but with red, white and blue predominant, as was to be expected. It was an impressive sight to behold, I must admit, even for one like me who did not reckon much of the whole thing, and whatever I reckoned then I reckon less now.

Some of the Irish people were flattered when the workmen who were putting up the flags obligingly tied a green one to their window. In my eyes they were only showing solidarity with the dying British empire, although I suppose they would not see it like that. For my part I felt I had more in common with the Donegal man McGinlay in Crown Street who pulled down every flag they put in his window, green or any other colour. He got done for causing a nuisance and breach of the peace and spent the week in the clink. That was one man who found out that his home was not his castle.

A big football event, the Coronation Cup, was put on specially for the occasion and was won by Celtic. That was a few days before the coronation. Pints were easy to get in some of the pubs that night with all the jubilant fans celebrating and the drink flowed even more freely on the great day itself. Publicans who spent the rest of their lives before and since giving short measures stood a round on the house for all and sundry that day. We had a paid holiday from our work, a thing that at any other time would have broken the hearts of some of the contractors. With no television on which to watch the momentous event the women contented themselves by listening to it on the radio. The men went out and got canned. Next day it was all in the papers; they issued several extra pages filled with descriptions and pictures of all the razzmatazz.

Bands played in the open air that night and people made bonfires and danced in the streets. Old men and women who had not danced for years and who would never dance again danced around the bonfires that night. And if they had any sense they would not have been dancing then either. Predaceous and rapacious whores and pickpockets did a roaring trade off the drunks while the police looked the other way. I stayed out late and next morning I was not able to get up for work. I felt as if I was about to die with a splitting sore head, and wretching to vomit, and nausea. I was not able to look at a bit of food, never mind keep it down. When I finally did get up and go out and about I found I was not the only one who had not gone to work. Sally O'Kane said it would not be a good thing if there was a coronation every day.

CHAPTER TWENTY

Strange Lodgings

AT ONE STAGE I WAS working near Dumbarton in a place called Dalria along the Helensburgh road. And so I thought it would be handy to be living near my work and to save myself three hours travelling every day. I left great value on one and a half hours extra sleep in the mornings; it was the difference of getting up at seven o'clock instead of half-past five and that was why I moved down there. But it was a move I soon came to regret. I did not like Dumbarton. It was a dead backwater of an old place and for the while I was there I came up to Glasgow every Saturday night for a drink in the pubs and in the places I was used to.

The lodgings was a bungalow in the town's west end—a house that had seen better days. The landlady was tallish and slenderish, and fortyish, with long peroxide blond hair, and that hair was her pride and joy. She used to sit for ages on a rug on the floor in front of the living room fire at night, combing it. She asked me what did I think of it the very first evening when I came in for my tea. I told her it was lovely and that must have pleased her; she put a cream tart on the plate. She was a good tart herself by all accounts. "Cold soup, hot woman", said one of the Poles who slept in the other room, and that summed it up well. Too hot for her husband; he had moved out, leaving her with a surely teenager son who spent his evenings taking his bike apart and putting it back together again; he had ambitions to be a mechanic one day. Also, she had a big grey tom cat which she nursed in her lap a lot of the time, and an old senile mother who lived in the attic and never came down the stairs. Well, hardly ever. She made an attempt one evening and had nearly reached the bottom before she was pushed and bundled back up again by her daughter and grandson. And she never got up in the morning to make the breakfasts like a landlady should. Provender in the shape of cornflakes, etc. were left on the table overnight and it was every man help himself and the early bird caught the early worm—the first man up had the best breakfast. I was the last man in getting up. When I left the house at seven-thirty there was still no sign of the landlady.

One of the lodgers was reputed to be sleeping with her. To be honest about it I do not know whether he slept with her or not and I did not care. That was up to himself and to her. He did not sleep in our room anyhow wherever he slept. I think he may have been the cock lodger all right, he was the favourite anyhow. I do not know where the other favourite, the cat, spent his nights either. I was always afraid he would prowl around and get up on the table during the night, but as far as I know he never did, not while I was there, and he was not to be seen in the morning. He must have been kept somewhere out of mischief's way.

Besides myself and the Isle of Skye man who shared the double bed with me, the other occupant of the room was an elderly man who slept in a single bed under the window; a labourer in the gas works who was also away from his wife; he was a local man with family married about the town. On the first Friday night, he came in about midnight with a half bottle of wine and some screwtops of beer which he sat up most of the night drinking. He woke me up to give me some of it, seeing as he said, that I was a new man in the town, but in reality I think, because he wanted someone to talk to, and drunk and all as he was he was wise enough to know the other man could not be bothered with him. Few things are more sickening than to have to sit awake at night listening to the silly ramblings of a drunk man. It was all right for him, he was not going out working in the morning. I could not get back to sleep again. He was still in bed and sleeping when I came in from my work at noon next day after him being the cause of me losing my night's sleep. When I mentioned the matter to him he said he did not remember a thing about it. Maybe he didn't.

He got something to remember the evening his wife landed up on the doorstep demanding money—a hard-looking old battleaxe of a woman. She was not sober by the sound of her, and she had a tongue that would be the envy of any navvy. Evidently he had fallen behind with his maintenance payments and when she had a few drinks in her she came round to remind him of it. He tried to calm her down. "Go easy", he was telling her, "people are listening." And they were; you could see the faces behind the curtains at the windows across the street, not to speak of us inside, peeping and listening to hear what went on, and if we never wanted to hear it we could not help but hear it for as the tempo of the discourse increased so too did the volume.

When his advice to her to tone down had the opposite effect from what it was meant to, he started saying something about what Jessie the daughter would do when she found out. "Fuck you and fuckin' Jessie", shouted his enraged and estranged spouse. "Jessie has a man to look after her, I have nae fuckin' man." After a while she went away, banging the gate loudly behind her. It was over for that time. He was very quiet for a few days after that; it took him the most part of a week to get back to his old self again.

Back again in Glasgow my place of residence for a time was an establishment owned and run by a big Englishwoman, one of the biggest women I ever knew. She was so big and manlike in appearance one would be excused for doubting if she was a woman; she was more like a man dressed in women's clothes. But she was a woman all right; she had a daughter nearly as big as herself but not as masculine looking—more rounded off, you will know what I mean—and a grand-daughter, two big women and a big gangling lassie.

There was nothing over-large about the dinners one or the other of them took in to the room to us on a tray—a new thing to me, this eating in the bedroom. In other places where I stayed we had always had our meals in the kitchen or in the living room. Six of us slept and ate in that big corner room with the small table in the middle of the floor and the six cot beds along the wall. At least each man had a bed to himself there, not like other digs where beds had to be shared.

The only times her man let us know he was in the house was on Saturday nights when he came in well-oiled after the pubs closing. Then he would collar me in the hall when I came in, shaking hands and telling me mysterious things that I did not understand. He came into the room to us a few times on Saturday nights, shaking hands; he was an awful man for the handshaking when he had the drink taken. And he did not just shake hands and leave it at that, he kept repeating the performance and yapping away at the same time in his cockney accent, so unintelligible to me he might as well be speaking Dutch as far as I was concerned. Meet him at any other time of the week and he did not have a word to say—would not let on that he knew you. The drink loosened his tongue. It turned him into a harmless nuisance.

The son-in-law, a clerk in some office up the town, was smaller and more refined than either his womenfolk or his foundry worker father-in-law. He looked out of place among them. He more or less ignored the presence of the lodgers; in fact I think he more or less ignored everybody in the house. And the lodgers kept coming and going. And as quick as they went others came to replace them until before long I was the longest lodger who had been there and then I started thinking about moving too.

I went to a house in the lower end of Crown Street to look for digs. The woman had a vacant place all right as I had heard earlier in the day that she had, but the snag was she only had busmen—corporation transport employees, three of them, and she was not so keen on taking in a labourer to the room with them. However, I must have made a good impression on her (it was Sunday and I was wearing my new suit), and so it came to pass that I became the fourth man in the room with the two bus conductors and the driver, or should I have said the driver and the two conductors, for that driver considered himself a step before and above the conductors. They were only doing a lassie's job, he reckoned. It took a man to drive one of those new trolley buses.

We got on gallantly together, the four of us, in that room. The one annoying thing to me, but through no fault of theirs, was that due to the staggered shifts they worked one or other of them was always going out very early in the morning or coming in very late at night. One might come in from his work at one o'clock in the morning and a couple of hours later another was rising for the early shift. And of course the noise of the coming and the goings and the switching on and off of the lights never failed to waken me up. And when I woke up at an unearthly hour it was the devil and all for me to go back to sleep again. Then if I did go to sleep I got it hard to wake up at my right time and I was groggy for half the day after it.

The youngest of the three, a teenager from Manorhamilton, County Leitrim, was my bed-mate. Tom was his name. He never went out to start on the early shift without banging doors, pulling drawers open and shut, and generally making the maximum amount of noise possible for such an occasion. And whenever he came in late he was quiet, slipped into bed as noiseless as a mouse. He said himself he was always "in bad order in the morning and tired at night". The landlady said he was "doing it out of sheer badness, to upset the rest of ye's because he has to get up". "He makes a wild noise, no need for the half of it", commented the Donegal man, the driver. Apart from the racket he made in the mornings Tom was not a bad lad. He liked to brag about all the frolics he was having with conductresses

172

around the back of Newton Mearns bus station. If the half of what he said was true it must have been an awful stud of a place. No wonder he was tired at night.

This woman did not get up to make breakfasts for the busmen but she was always up at seven o'clock before I left. She was a grass widow, or a deserted wife, or whatever is the way to describe the likes of her. Her man had "piked off" as she put it, and started another family with another woman, "a young bit of stuff" up the road in Govanhill. "And I cannot get a penny out of the old bastard. Sometimes I feel like going after him and giving him a sherricking", she declared. (That was what the woman in Dumbarton had done.) She and he must have stayed together a good while; they had a big family, seven in all, all grown up by then, three of them married and one separated.

I wonder what it is that sometimes causes a middle-aged or elderly man to forsake the security of marriage, home and family in order to go off and shack up with a younger woman. Whatever it is I hope it doesn't happen to me.

CHAPTER TWENTY-ONE

Sinn Féin

IT WAS MY INCREASINGLY IRISH nationalistic and radical ways of thinking that led to me becoming a member of Sinn Féin. Three branches of the organisation functioned openly and without hindrance in the Glasgow area at that time. They were: the James Connolly cumann in the south side; the Barnes and McCormick cumann in Dennistoun; and the Liam Mellows cumann in Clydebank. I became a member of the James Connolly cumann, proposed by the late Emily Hyland and seconded by the late Phil Jordan in my application for membership.

I always had a political awareness ever since I was very young. When I was at school I was de Valera daft. I had his picture, cut from his party's paper, the *Irish Press*, stuck on to the wall beside my bed. Partly from conviction and partly to torment some of my old neighbours who were anti-de Valera, I used to go around singing, or rather shouting, because I was never able to sing, a verse about him that I heard somewhere.

Up de Valera, the captain of the fight,
We will follow him to battle with the yellow, green and white.
We'll follow him to battle, and we'll fight at his command,
And we'll crown de Valera, King of Ireland.

And then I would shout: "Up the Republic"—after shouting about crowning a king!

But gradually I changed. I think it was the time Darcy and McNeela died in jail on hunger strike that started it off. That was the first time ever I heard my father say anything against the Fianna Fáil government. It was when the news got out about the harsh treatment that had been meted to them, the prisoners. He was a humane and sensitive man by nature and anything like that was repellent to him, as it is to me also—to read about people in custody being beaten to

174

get confessions out of them. And make no mistake, more of it goes on than is ever admitted, and the Irish, when they get a bit of power in their hands are no more immune from behaving in that way than any other race. Anyhow, my father changed his mind about the sanctity of the Fianna Fáil administration at a time when I was at an impressionable age and that must have helped to change me too. Or did I change? I would like to feel that I never changed, that it was others who did the changing. I always tried to keep to what I believed to be the straight path.

The first political party I became a member of was Clann na Poblachta in 1948. The leader of that party was Seán MacBride, the son of Mayo man John MacBride, who was executed by the British in 1916, and of Maud Gonne, a woman who was a renowned patriot and benefactor in her own right. MacBride was a good man, but to my way of thinking, one of his colleagues, a young medical doctor named Noel Browne, was a better man. Browne was not as nationally-minded as MacBride, but he was stronger on social issues. He was a man with a burning ambition—to do something about the health of the people—and he soon got a chance to put his talk into action. He was made Minister of Health on his very first day in the Dáil under the new coalition government. He was then thirty-two years of age.

Tuberculosis was the dreaded plague and scourge in Ireland at that time. It was rampant all over the country often wiping out whole families, more especially young women and girls. Browne himself had personal experience of its devastations; it had killed his parents and other members of his family and nearly killed himself, leaving him almost a semi-invalid. It was his fervent determination to be able to work to combat the disease that gave him the strength to persevere in spite of ill health until he qualified as a doctor, and that was what prompted him to enter politics. He proved to be a remarkable politician if ever there was one. Seldom, I believe, in Ireland or anywhere else, did any man ever pursue a crusade with such dedication and success as did that frail young man. He was unusual for a politician because not only did he talk about getting things done, he actually got things done. Within the space of a few years as a minister his work had virtually rid the country of TB and that was one of the greatest achievements ever of any man in Ireland. He fought disease and ill health on every front regardless of what it cost in money. Nothing was too big for him to undertake nor too small to overlook. He got new hospitals built and he cleaned up and modernised the old hospitals. He opened the gates and the doors of the mental hospitals and brought them into the twentieth century. But it was all to good to last.

Browne was not well-liked in certain well-heeled circles. He was moving too fast. A lot of what he was doing did not win the approval of the conservative-minded Catholic bishops or of the Irish Medical Association. Scrapping the means test, giving people free choice of doctors, or any form of sex education; those were things they did not want to hear mentioned. Matters came to a head when he introduced, or rather re-introduced, the Mother and Child Scheme to give free medical help to mothers and young children. It had been drafted before by the de Valera government, but when Dr McQuaid, the Archbishop of Dublin, stuck his nose in and put the pressure on, it was dropped. But now they were up against a different kettle of fish, now they were dealing with a man who was not going to be dictated to by any bishop; he was one of the few men in Irish politics who ever had the courage to tell them to mind their own business. But he was up against it too. There is more than one way of skinning a cat. If they could not get Browne one way they could get him another way. And they did.

Some of the bishops got at some of the other coalition ministers and put the wind up them. They panicked and refused to go along with the Mother and Child Scheme with the result the coalition split: MacBride, in order to try and save the government, backed down, which he should not have done. Browne was left in the lurch and forced to resign, and though he remained in the Dáil for over thirty years, because in spite of everything the people continued to vote for him, he never again held government office. Thus it was clearly shown who wielded the real power in the Irish Republic; not the elected representatives of the people, but the fellas with the croziers. That burst-up brought about the end of Clann na Poblachta.

A branch of Fianna Fáil existed in Glasgow in the late fourties and early fifties. The big chief himself, de Valera, or "Davie" as his adoring adherents called him (I never heard him called by that name only by the Donegal people in Glasgow), came over to see them and, I suppose, to give them moral support. And they were as proud-looking as anything, posing with him for the cameras, so as to get their pictures into the newspapers. I could not help wondering when I saw them if some of them who had been members of the

176

Glasgow police force at one time would not have turned him in had they caught him thirty years before when he was a fugitive on the run in this city. I bet they would not have been so anxious to get themselves photographed in his company then. They would have been happier to see him in handcuffs, I'll wager. But a man can change and so did Dev. He was a respectable man now. He no longer had any truck with Sinn Féin. I never heard of Fine Gael having any branches in Scotland.

All three Sinn Féin branches were very active, holding meetings, ceilidhies and concerts. Members trudged around the Irish pubs selling the republican paper, the *United Irishman*, and collecting for prisoners' aid and other related things. We were regarded as a bad nuisance or worse by Fianna Fáil and others who were very tame and pro-establishment minded as are their successors to this very day. But we kept going.

Sinn Féin had a cultural and a social side to it as well as a political side. "Shoneenism" would not be tolerated at any of its functions. Dancing, songs, etc. had to be traditionally Irish and we had Irish language classes and Irish drama groups. All in all, a lot of Sinn Féin activity took place in Glasgow and other parts of Scotland at that time, far more than is known about now.

Tom Doyle, the national president of the organisation, a lineal successor to Griffith and de Valera, came over from Dublin a few times and stayed the weekend, giving pep talks to the assembled faithful in the afternoons and addressing public meetings in halls at night. Tall, sparse, bespectacled, Doyle, a man of school teacherish mien, did not at all look the flamboyant type one might connect with his IRA exploits of some years previous. He was a quiet spoken man, without airs or graces. I remember him telling us that he was often tempted to pack it all in. It was only the thought of the people who had gone before him, of the men and women who had sacrificed everything, even their very lives for the cause; he could not let them down, and so he would go on, fighting the republican struggle to the end. And that, he said, was what all true republicans should do. Cathal Brugha had said that if there was only one man left, and if that man was down on the ground and the enemy standing over him with their bayonets raised, ready to drive them into his body, and he was asked to forsake the cause, even then he should say, "No". I was not sure I agreed with that. I am afraid if ever I found myself in that position I would be all for saving myself, whatever about the cause.

177

One night soon after that I was discussing Cathal Brugha with one of the Glasgow-born members of Sinn Féin, and I thought it was funny how he kept pronouncing the name as "Cackle Broogia". The man's name in English was, of course, Charles Burgess. I left Sinn Féin in the early nineteen-sixties for reasons over which I will not go into detail. Enough to say I disagreed with certain points of party policy. Many of the old members are gone now, but some are still happily with us. I remained on good terms with them over the years. This much I can say without hesitation: they were good people to know.

CHAPTER TWENTY-TWO

A Holiday Romance

FOR THE SUMMER HOLIDAYS OF 1954 I returned home for a fortnight. I met Pat Conroy in the booking office and we travelled together the whole way to Belmullet. We met some nice Donegal girls on the Derry boat that night and their company helped to shorten the journey. I corresponded with one of them for a long time afterwards, and I still have the picture of herself that she gave me, after all these years, even though I only met her twice altogether. Her name was Roisín; she was from Rathmullan, and she worked as a shorthand typist in Derry. She was on her way back after a holiday with relatives in Jordonhill in the west end of Glasgow. In ways she was like myself—interested in history and reading—that sort of thing, so there was much we were able to talk about and before we parted we arranged to meet again on my way back.

On landing in the early hours of the morning, everybody I think who had been on the boat hastened to one or other of two restaurants: Molloy's or Sweeney's, both of whom had touts down at the quay, shouting to make sure we knew they were open for business. "Breakfast in Con Molloy's." "Early breakfasts now being served in Sweeney's."

It was about eight o'clock that evening by the time we reached Belmullet, having changed buses twice, in Sligo and in Ballina. We had been travelling all day but we never felt the time passing; talking about one thing or another, about the things we would do in the fortnight out before us, and the girls we might find in addition to the two we had found on the boat, and so on, and the time fairly flew.

It was the fifteenth of July and there had been a fair in the town that day, as there always was, and still is, on the fifteenth of every month. The cattle had left such a mess after them on the street, I remember I got it hard to keep my new shoes from getting dirty. Talk had long been going on of the advisability of holding the fairs in a field outside the town but it never got past the talking stage. The shopkeepers were all in favour of retaining the status quo, in other words, leaving things the way they were. They were quite happy to suffer the animal dung on the street for a day once a month as long as the money kept coming in, for they knew full well that to take the fair away out to a field would not be good for trade. The fairday was their peak day every month for business.

Mary Jo was waiting at the bus stop outside Agnes Gaughan's. The three of us, Pat Conroy, Mary Jo and myself, went into John Doherty's and there we met Pat Carey, a neighbour from Morahan who was home on holidays from Edinburgh. Pat was a widower: his wife, a young woman, had died suddenly some years before. He was a grand man and a born comedian. My mother used to say, "poor Pateen Carey would make the cat laugh", he was so funny. God rest their souls, they are all dead now.

Old John Doherty took us down to Morahan in his hackney car. My father and mother saw us coming and were out at the gate to meet us. Mother looked well I thought, but Dad had aged a lot. He kissed me, which was not like him; he had never been one to show outward signs of affection. His hand, when he shook mine, was hard and rough, as was his face, and well I knew what had done that to him. It was the lifetime of work, fighting for a livelihood on field and mountain and shore, against the harsh climate of the western seaboard.

Pat Walsh came in and we drank a few bottles of stout. I walked down the road with him when he was leaving. It would have been well past midnight by then, a lovely clear summer's night in the middle of July. I remember it well and how we stood talking for a while, and the peace and the serenity of the place. There, in the silence of the bright night, in the stillness of the countryside, with no noise to be heard only that of our own voices and the low constant murmur of the sea and the barking of a dog in the distance, one could feel close to the creator: the stars of the heavens seemed so near you would think you could almost touch them.

I felt that night that I had missed out a lot on having been away from home. I felt sorry for my father, hacked and hard and weather-beaten; past his best, on the decline. He had crossed over the top of the hill of life and was now going down on the other side. Had I failed him? It was a thought that had troubled me before and would do so again, many times. Should not I, his son, be at home with him as he had been with his father, helping him now when he was getting older, taking some of the load off his back, making things a bit easier for him? That I knew was what he had hoped for from me but I had not lived up to his expectations.

On the other hand did I not have the right to be my own man, to go my own road, make my own way in the world, and in time to marry and set up a home of my own, independent of my parents? It was as if I was being pulled in opposite directions, torn between two feelings. To follow in my father's footsteps did not always appeal to me; his life was not an easy one, he never knew many of the comforts of this world. He had the little piece of land which he could call his own and in the end he left it to me though he knew I had chosen to live far away from it. He left me all he had and no man could do more for his son than that.

On Saturday night I was in the town and I met Pat Conroy and Pat Carey and another man, Lavelle, and we had a few drinks together in McDonnell's. People shook hands asking what part of England had we been in. Always it was "England" with them—no word about Scotland. We left McDonnell's about midnight and went down to Forty's and we were not long there when two Guards came in and chased away the locals. We were OK they told us; we were bona fide, and so we could drink on, meaning that as we lived more than three miles away, we were travellers and therefore entitled to a drink after hours. And what do you think the Guards did once they got the others away? They came into the bar for a drink with us, and not only one drink, we had several drinks before we left, and the two men in uniform were as canned as any of us. It was a good old night.

On Sunday night a crowd of us went in Anthony Munnelly's car to the dance in Walsh's hall in Drum. About ten of us cramped into the old car that night. It was not a comfortable ride. The first place we went to was W.B. Padden's for a drink. Some of the lads made out they would be better at chatting up the girls when they had a few drinks in them—it would give them "courage" they reckoned. And again the Guards raided, but this time they did not come in to drink with us. We were herded out to the turfhouse while they were at the door and there we huddled in the darkness until they went away. They were not supposed to serve drink on the Sunday at that time. It was by the hall door we had been let in as the main door was closed. I think the Guards knew fine about us being there but they were not too keen to catch either us or the publican. Then when we were leaving we were sent out a different way, out the back door into the lane.

The dance was far advanced by the time we got there. I made an attempt to "square up" a big lassie from Gladree but she told me coldly that I had "an awful smell of drink" off me and that got no farther than that. None of us got fixed up with a woman that night except the driver, Munnelly. He got one and went away with her, and left us standing around outside the hall for ages after the dance was over, waiting for him to come back, whatever it was they were doing up the road in the car. Some claimed they knew but I am not going to say now what it was.

The fortnight passed and then came the day when it was time for me to go again. I remember the morning well, as good as I do today. For the two weeks I was there I had not been idle, helping with the hay and bringing home the turf. We had a good stack at the back of the house so they would have a warm fire when the winter came. The hay was in cocks in the garden but was not built into a reek. Sonny Padden would come on a fine day and help him to do that.

Paddy McAndrew arrived in his car to drive me into town to catch the bus. My father left the field where he was minding the cows to come up to the road and see me off. He looked dejected and had little to say. My mother cried. Mary Jo asked me to come again at Christmas. Once the car moved off I cried too.

I resolved that morning on the bus that I would be back again at the end of the year and this time it would be for good. It was seven years since that other fine morning when I went away with the potato squad. Seven and a half years was enough; now maybe I should settle myself at home. In years to come I would be able to talk about when I was in Scotland working with the builders around Glasgow the same as the old men I had often listened to as a boy, telling about the times when they worked in the pits around Hamilton, or on the making of the railways. My father had never been outside County Mayo in his life and God knows there was a time when I used to look down on him for it, because of his non-experience of the country across the water. Now I was seeing things in a different light. Was my father not as good a man as many of those who had been away? He was certainly a better man than ever I was. He had stayed at home in his own country and never deserted it or went away from it; he has stuck it out through thick and thin and made a living at home. I would do the same, or so I thought at the time, but it did not work out that way.

The first thing I did in Derry was to find a bed and breakfast place and having booked in for the night I then went to see Roisín, the girl

182

I met on the boat, at the address she had given me of her lodgings in the Waterside. She was just in from her work and was expecting me and while she got ready to go out with me I sat nervously on a chair being quizzed by her landlady while a pair of equally curious children silently took stock of me as well.

I would have liked to have gone for a drink but Roisín, being a Pioneer, would not go into a pub, never mind be seen drinking in one, so we went for a walk instead. She wanted to show me the old city walls and I recall we went to some part from where we could see down the Foyle and west across to the Donegal hills where her home lay. She was a lovely, intelligent, pure-minded girl with an intense sense of history and it was good to be in her company—too good for one like me. It was beautiful in Derry on the summer's evening, and by my side the winsome dark haired colleen I had met on the Derry boat and who belonged not to Derry but to Donegal over the border, a border she definitely thought should not be there and so did I.

I slept well that night and next evening Roisín came down to the quay with me. She wished she was going to Glasgow as she had enjoyed it thoroughly when she was there, especially the Locarno dance hall. I had never been to the Locarno. I never saw Roisín again though we wrote to each other for a long time, even after I went home, and even after I came back again to Glasgow. She is probably long years ago married and her family reared.

CHAPTER TWENTY-THREE

Going Home

I WAS WORKING WITH Shanks & MacEwan on the building of East Kilbride new town. Another man who started there on the same day as I did was an Indian, the only Indian I think ever I worked beside on a job, and he was a nice man. He bore the funny-sounding name of Ram. "And I bet he is a right old ram", said Highland man Duncan Gillies. The ganger asked him was Ram his Christian name or his surname. Poor Ram was not a christian at all but a Hindu, though come to think of it, it would have been good if the Christians were all like him. He was a better Christian in his own way than some of us who called ourselves Christians. He was a good fellow who laughed about our fooling and took no offence at the silly and stupid things we said. We called him "John Ram". He was as nice and harmless a man as ever I worked beside.

The old site agent was Jimmy Wright. "Right by name and wrong by nature" was one of the comments I heard used about him. Wright was a crabbit old man, fussing about the way the concrete was laid down and that sort of thing. One day he went into the hut complaining that he was not feeling well. The nipper, a worthy who answered to the name of Lambert, made tea for him, and after drinking it he sat down and died, just like that, there on the bench in the hut. Lambert got teased plenty about it afterwards, making out that he poisoned the agent. Of course there was no such thing; the man died from a natural cause—a massive heart attack.

Then a new agent came and he had his own clique with him. Duncan left shortly afterwards. I hung on for a while and then I left, myself and a Galway man named Willie Burke, and we started down the road with Wimpey. The same Willie Burke was often slagged because his name was unfortunately the same as that of another Irishman who was hanged in Edinburgh early in the nineteenth century. He, along with his mate Willie Hare, have come down in Scottish folklore as the "grave robbers", but they were not grave robbers; they were mass murderers who suffocated their victims to death and then sold their bodies to the anatomists to practise on. This Willie Burke I knew was a decent man and he could no more help having the name of a mass murderer than I could help having the surname of an informer.

Wimpey's had been my employer twice before, though not at East Kilbride, and now I was back for the third and last time. Tim Tynan, nicknamed "Tipperary Tim" after the county of his origin, said when he was taking my cards, "I suppose you won't be staying long." I thought I might as well be honest with the man. "I don't suppose I will", I replied. But that did not stop Tim from putting me to work. And East Kilbride was a mucky place to work in, in wintertime or any time.

The site foreman, the big chief, who was over Tim and the others, was an Englishman named Joe Watson, an awful greedy man for work. One of the navvy gangers, not the one I was sent to work under, was for some reason known to everyone as "the moocher". I never heard him referred to by his right name which was Sweeney, but always as "the moocher". I never saw the man doing any mooching— a slang word for cadging, going around asking people for things—nor did I ever hear anybody else saying they saw him doing it. Still, there must have been some reason for giving him a name like that. Nicknames always had something at the back of them.

Some men who worked with Wimpey for a spell at one time or another give a bad account of their foremen and gangers— rascals, one and all, they will tell you. I could not honestly say that I found them any worse than their counterparts elsewhere. The thing I found wrong with them most was that they had been too long with the firm; they did not know anywhere else, and many of them had reached the stage where they thought they could not be done without. Well, they were done without. All of them are dead and gone or long retired now and Wimpey is still going strong. There is not a word about them any more as if they had never been with the firm. Once they thought they were indispensable but now they are gone, unmissed and unlamented; as the poet said, "unwept, unhonoured and unsung".

A thing I had against Wimpey's was the way they made us work out in all kinds of weather: no such thing as getting rained off on a bad day. We were supplied with oilskins but they were bad oilskins, often a jacket with only one sleeve or trousers with only one leg. Any man who did not like it could go. We were told a drop of rain never melted any man. Well, if it did not melt him, it came against him in other ways in the course of time. I saw Wimpey's old-timers going around, limping and lop-sided, half crippled with rheumatism and other related ailments through working out in the rain. And the man who done strenuous work all day wearing waterproofs would be almost as wet on the inside from sweat and condensation as he would from the rain if he went without them. I for one do not think the human body will stand that kind of thing for long. It might stand it for a while but sooner or later it will get the man down.

In December I went home with the intention of staying at home. The Leitrim man MacGowan I talked to in Glasgow the night before I left said he wished he had my chance and if he had he would do the same. Once he could have done so but he did not; he had put down his roots here now and here he must remain. He was married to a Scotswoman and, "enough said", there would be no going back to a small farm in Leitrim with her. We talked as we sipped our beer in the Cumberland Arms that night about the grants which, according to the Irish papers, were so freely available over there to anyone with a bit of land. Grants for land reclamation, for drainage, for levelling out old ditches and fences, and for many other things too. "Money for old boots", said the Leitrim man. And good money for turf. Anyone with bogs was on a Klondyke. Well, that was one thing we had in plenty—bogs. I used to think at one time there was enough bogland on the commonage of Morahan to keep every family in the townland in turf, both for their own use and for selling, until the end of time.

I might have a go at all those things. I might have a go at a lot of things but I knew well in my own mind that while I lived under my father's roof and worked on his land, never, while he was able, would I be the one to handle the purse. That would be for him, and who could blame him? After all, the land was his. Let that be as it may I felt I had enough of life in Scotland, digging muck by day and longing for each day to pass, and at night often walking the streets until bedtime rather than sit in a half-freezing room. "We're only wishing our lives away here", said the Leitrim man as he studied the diminishing contents of his beer glass.

I felt the same way myself at that particular time, but unlike him I was able to do something about it. There was nothing to keep me from going home, to sit at our own fire or at a neighbour's fire enjoying the crack in the winter nights and without any worry about getting up early to go out working. Ireland had things in its favour. It was a place where if people saw you before nine o'clock in the morning you were an early riser. No getting up at six o'clock there! It was the place where people did not rush and hurry the whole time. I was going home.

CHAPTER TWENTY-FOUR

Farewell to Mayo

AFTER A SIXTEEN-HOUR VOYAGE down the Irish sea and a bus journey across Ireland I found myself once more in Belmullet. It rained I think nearly the whole way. Pat Carolan of Glencastle was on the bus on his way home from England where he had been at the beet pulling, and he had with him as part of his luggage a bicycle, "all the way from Lincoln". Pat must have been an unconventional man as regards the things he carried on public transport. There was a story that one year coming home from the beet he bought a ram in Mullingar and managed to take the animal the whole way to Glencastle by bus. He told me that day that he crossed to England to work at the beet every year for over forty years without a break; some years he went to England twice—to the hoeing in summer, came home and gathered his harvest, and went again to the pulling at the back-end. Always it was the beet. "Tried public works once and didn't like it; money no good."

We never felt the time passing, talking about one thing or another. "Are you coming in for a drink, Anthony?" He was confusing my father's name with mine. The driver assured us he would not go without us. You would never get personal attention like that from bus drivers in Glasgow. Over there if you weren't exactly at the stop they would run right past and leave you there. "We are in God's country now", said Pat.

We had about an hour's delay in Longford and after that it did not seem long until we pulled into Ballina. It is very true that having a good story-teller for company on a journey can shorten the road. We had another drink in Mike Gaughan's in Ballina and this time the bus could not very well go without us because the driver, Tom Cuffe, was in the pub with us. Tom was a nice man. He and Pat were well acquainted from many bus journeys.

From Ballina westwards it was very dark. Old Peter Walsh of Attycunnane was in the seat in front of us and he kept talking across his shoulder, stabbing towards the window with his pipe and emitting tobacco smoke which tormented my eyes and went down my windpipe. But Peter took no notice of my spluttering, he just carried on with his smoking and with his running commentary, naming such and such a townland and such and such a house as we passed through Crossmolina and Corick and Bangor and headed towards Belmullet. As a county council ganger of long standing he was a much travelled man all about the area, but all I could see was the light of a window here and there. Peter knew the countryside well. This was Cosgrove's house and this was Gibbons' house, he was saying. I mentioned that I once knew a Shiela Gibbons from around there, a nice girl. "You're too late if it's her you're thinking about", old Peter informed me. She was married now, he said, "well married" to a school teacher "from down the country far", meaning not Cork or Kerry but probably some townland in the next parish.

In Belmullet, my father, my mother, and Mary Jo were waiting for me, the first and only time ever I knew the three of them to turn out to meet me. We went home in Seamus Murphy's car. I was home now to stay, I thought. I took out the three hundred pounds I had in the Bank and bought a second-hand Ford car from Jack McLaughlinn of Belmullet. The car cost me two hundred and forty and it took the other sixty pounds to tax and insure it. I thought then that I was a made man, that I would be able to make a living doing hackney work the same as Henaghan and those other blokes were doing, and help my father on the land at the same time. But I did not foresee nor take account of all the bills I would be paying to garages for repairs. I was useless in that line, still am. Not in a million years would I learn to do my own car repairs.

McLaughlinn, like every used car dealer ever I knew, had ambitions to be a rogue. He fancied himself as a professional conman but he was only a small town, small time performer. He would not have made a clerk for some of the conmen I have come across. I know he will not take offence at me for saying that about him now. He cannot, because he is long dead and gone. I suppose he was doing his best at the conning game and nobody can do any more than their best. He was not a bad fellow really.

The car took me around. It took me into every townland in the barony and into every town in the county. For the next two years I drove hackney in Erris and around Mayo. I took the old people to the town to collect their pensions, the youngsters to the dance halls, and the devout to Knock Shrine. I took emigrants to the bus and railway stations when they were leaving, and I took the holiday-makers around to visit friends and places of interest. For a while I drove the pension officer to interview his clients, not the snappy little man who had interviewed me about the dole when I was eighteen, but another man, a younger man—a Kerryman named Buckley who for some reason did not have a car of his own. I found him to be a very likeable man although everybody did not say that about him. I suppose he would have to be an angel to please them all. Sometimes I drove along the road to Ballina in front of the bus and picked up its would-be passengers on the way much to the chargin of an officious conductor called Tony something: I forget his surname, not that it matters much anyhow. Tom Cuffe never minded me picking up the odd passenger for myself. I did other poaching too a few times in the river around Corick at night. My part in that was to act as look-out man on the river bank while two others dragged the salmon pools with a net.

And I picked the oysters and the winkles as of old as well as helping my father on the land and on the bog at the turf or the peat as they call it in Scotland. Looking back now, I think those were the two busiest years I ever had and the two hardest years ever I worked and I had nothing to show for it all at the end of it.

The bad roads and the heavy loads took their toll on my hackney car. Hardly a day passed but something was giving way in it. If if wasn't broken springs it was torn tyres and if it wasn't that it was something else and no sooner was one thing fixed or replaced than another thing went wrong. And when you don't know half the time what the trouble is never mind know how to fix it you are at the mercy of the man in the garage and garagemen were not noted for their scruples then any more than now. Every penny I earned with the car went into its upkeep and when it was jiggered I did not have the money to buy another. I sold it to John Connor of Crossmolina for just enough to pay my way back to Scotland. Some men made a success out of hackney work: I was not able to.

During the two years and a bit more that I had been away the winds of change had been blowing through the Gorbals. My aunt, Mrs Gallagher, and her family had like many of their neighbours been moved out to newly-built Castlemilk on the slopes of Cathkin Braes and it was to there I made my way as I had gone to their home in Florence Street nearly ten years before. With them I would always be sure of a welcome and a meal and they would be glad to see me and to hear the news from Ireland. That afternoon I set out to look for a place to live and after a few disappointments I found one, a small attic room in Cathcart Road and there I remained until I got married two years later.

Luck was with me in that I got a job without delay even if it was only digging a sewer to serve the needs of Ibrox football ground, for it was not a good time of year and my money was nearly gone. I left Ibrox and went back to the old firm of R.W. Stewart a few weeks later when I heard they were starting work on the construction of an extension to Bearsden Veterinary College. Braidwood was on the site when I called and he remembered me from Rutherglen days and put me to work. The foreman was Willie Mathieson whom I had known before as an apprentice bricklayer. Bob Stewart was now dead and as he had left no issue the firm was being run by the triumvirate of Braidwood, Cobly and Smith, three men with whom, as I said before, I never had cause to find fault. For the next eighteen months or so I carried a three foot rule, a spirit level and a small trowel at my work, which was laying concrete edging and levelling out the ground around the extension—the only time I think I ever used any tools on a building site besides a pick and shovel. When that job was finished we were moved to work on Arden new shopping centre where we spent a few more months and then we were moved once again to the building of a scheme in Newton Mearns, a job on which there was neither overtime nor bonus, only the bare hours, with the result I packed in and started with MacTaggart and Mickel, and they were the last navvying firm I ever worked for.

Frank Mickel was a dour, dark-complexioned little man of fifty odd, known to his employees as "The Black Prince". Some of the old hands of the firm were very much afraid of him, more so than ever I had known men to be afraid of a contractor, and none acted more afraid than the two gangers, Paddy Judge and Tom Golden. Whether it was trying to scare us they were or not I don't know but whenever he was around they were almost like children terrified of a man whom they had been warned might take them away with him. That was what Fred Monaghan compared them to and it was a good comparison. Sometimes I had wished he would take them away with him. Mickel was not half as bad as they were making him out to be.

My marriage in 1959 brought to me added responsibilities and with them the incentive to seek for a more settled work-style. I had accepted the inevitable—a future of more or less permanent exile and I was on the look-out for a way of earning a living away from the building sites and the constant changing and moving from one contractor to another and from one job to the next.

It was in the *Evening Citizen* I saw the advert. It read: "Experienced Gardeners wanted. MacDonald Brothers. Nurserymen and Landscape Contractors. Muirend." My knowledge or experience of gardening, landscape or otherwise, was but very rudimentary. I had made the few extra bob a few times tidying up gardens in the evenings at the big houses near to where I worked as did others, but apart from that I knew practically nothing about gardening. Yet I figured out that if I could get into it full time it might be steadier for me than how I was and it was one of the few kinds of manual work I enjoyed doing.

I went to Muirend and had a word with Ronald MacDonald. I admitted that I had but little experience of the job. He asked me did I know how to cut grass with a scythe and when I told him I did he went into the shed and took out a scythe and a whetting stone and said to let him see me sharpen it. I sharpened the scythe as many a time I had seen my father and others do it and often attempted to do it myself. But that was the first time ever I was complimented on it. My father or his peers would not have thought much of me as a scythe sharpener. MacDonald thought different; he also thought that I was good at cutting with the scythe. He had about twenty men working for him and not one of them knew how to use a scythe. In the country of the blind the one-eyed man is king.

So that was how come I started with MacDonald Brothers and although I did not do that much scything for them altogether—three of four days around the neglected grounds of a factory—I was with them for near enough twelve years until I started up a garden service of my own. But that is another story.